Calypso Coolers

D1413748

Recipes for 50 Caribbean Cocktails and 20 Tropical Treats

Calypso
Coolers

Arlen Gargagliano   *Photographs by* Ellie Miller

Stewart, Tabori & Chang

NEW YORK

To Seth, Sofia, and Wes

Pictured on page 2 *(from left to right)*: Sorrel Champagne Cocktail, Dominica Lime Punch, Belize Cocktail

Published in 2006 by Stewart, Tabori & Chang
An imprint of Harry N. Abrams, Inc.

Text copyright © 2006 by Arlen Gargagliano
Editor: Jennifer Eiss
Designer: woolypear
Production Manager: Jacquie Poirier

Photographs copyright © 2006 by Ellie MIller
Food Stylist: Sara Neumeier
Prop Stylist: Karen Quatsoe
Photo Assistant: Brica Wilcox

Library of Congress Cataloging-in-Publication Data
Gargagliano, Arlen.
    Calypso coolers : recipes for 50 caribbean cocktails and 20 tropical
treats / by Arlen Gargagliano, photographs by Ellie Miller.
        p. cm.
    ISBN-13: 978-1-58479-569-8
    ISBN-10: 1-58479-569-7
        1. Cocktails—Caribbean Area. I. Title.
TX951.G24 2007
641.8'7409729--dc22   2006023067

The text of this book was composed in Barcelona.

Printed and bound in China
10 9 8 7 6 5 4 3 2 1

HNA
harry n. abrams, inc.
a subsidiary of La Martinière Groupe

115 West 18th Street
New York, NY 10011
www.hnabooks.com

CONTENTS

7   Introduction

11   Classic Caribbean Cocktails

27   Daiquiris & Tropical-Infused Cocktails

51   Martinis & Caribbean-Fruit Cocktails

71   Punches

101   Silky & Spirited

116   Acknowledgments

117   Conversion Charts

118   Index

INTRODUCTION

Your skin tingles as you gaze upon the crystal-clear waters of the Caribbean. A turquoise-blue sea sparkles in front of you, soft white sand cushions your toes, and willowy palms applaud above you. Warm breezes carry gentle perfumes of guava and coconut. As you lift your glass, the sweet aromas of fresh lemon and lime juice waft upward, and you gingerly sip your rum sour. Your companion takes a taste from a fresh pineapple-studded glass, brimming with the passion fruit and mango nectars of a Caribbean cocktail. You both smile. The caressing sun offers a delicious contrast to your luscious, chilled libations. No matter where you are, no matter what the season, *Calypso Coolers* conjures up the magic of tropical seaside ecstasy.

Local cocktails have been enchanting visitors to the Caribbean for years. Colorful and cheerful, like the area that gave birth to these delights, this collection of drinks—and accompanying snacks—captures that first-day-of-vacation feeling. These treats are enjoyed in the Colonial Zone in Santo Domingo, where you can hear a backdrop of merengue and conversation along with the clicking of the dominoes as players sit under palm-shaded tables. They're also relished in the towns and beaches that hug the edges of the Central American coast and those in the Lesser Antilles, all the way down to the streets of Port of Spain, where, come carnival time, revelers from around the world gather in the birthplace of Calypso music to rejoice on the boot-shaped island of Trinidad and its sister island, Tobago. Though the ingredients and locations may change, the various peoples of the Caribbean share a common belief: Being with people, taking the time to talk and play together, and relishing the beauty of nature's bounty is good for the soul. The recipes in this collection celebrate this philosophy.

Caribbean food is as varied and vibrant as the area's people and history. From the cool silky rum-and-coconut refreshments, to the crispy-on-the-outside, sexy-smooth-on-the-inside Puerto Rican Corn Sticks, this region of the world boasts a wonderful combination of flavors and textures. The rich mélange of Caribbean peoples—who live across thousands of islands, coastlines, and miles—are a combination of descendants of the Caribs, Taínos, and Arawaks (indigenous people of the region), slaves from Africa, laborers from China and India, colonists from Europe, and traders from the Middle East—to name just a few. Despite the fact that so many of today's Caribbean dwellers had ancestors who were brutally torn from their roots in distant lands and transplanted far, far away, there is a dynamic feeling of national pride among the area's residents, and a warm reaching-out to visitors, which easily seduces guests (and often keeps them there as new settlers). The cocktails, food, languages, and customs of this region reflect the heritage of its inhabitants, as well as its rich flora and fauna.

My first visit to the Caribbean took place when I was in first grade, when my family visited St. Thomas in the Virgin Islands. Vivid is the memory of the pristine waters that made it so easy to see fish that came in colors I had never before seen in nature. Equally alive is the memory of eating my first mango, after seeing a tree dripping with the kidney-shaped fruit in various stages of ripeness. That visit marked a first time for many new sights—and tastes. I remember sitting on the beach, under the shade of coconut palms, sipping that fresh fruit's water from nature's cup, and eating still-warm shredded-coconut cookies that gorgeous, brown-skinned women uncovered from cloth napkin-draped baskets they toted.

A couple of years later, we traveled to the beautiful island of Jamaica. Though I certainly recall chasing lizards and climbing Dunn's River Falls, my memories of the culinary component of that trip are even more stunning. It was there that

I first enjoyed plantains in many forms, including deliciously addictive Jamaican Banana Fritters (page 36) which my mom got from that visit and has made dozens of times since, as well as deep-red sorrel drinks, smooth orange-papaya concoctions, and new exotic fruits like soursop, guavas, and papayas—just to name a few. On our next trip we ventured to Puerto Rico where, in between visits to El Yunque and listening to the music of the coquís (tree frogs that have a unique and wonderful song!), my siblings and I gorged ourselves on what seemed to be endless amounts of pineapples, mangoes, and guavas—in addition to fried treats like *bacalaítos*—Codfish Cakes—(page 74), and *surullitos*, or Puerto Rican Corn Sticks (page 84).

Maybe it's the icy New York winters that inspire my Caribbean dreams, but I can't get the flavors and feelings of that region out of my mind. And I don't want to! Now I've tried to instill in my own children that lust for travel to places where a walk outside can yield a collection of freshly tree-picked tropical treats and a swim in a crystal-clear ocean that can reveal limitless shades of blue and green. I want them to meet people whose personal treasure chests contain diverse and richly woven histories that include thousands of miles and flavors—all fascinating and exotic, yet somehow familiar. Fortunately, we can start this journey right here at home; we've heard many a New York City cab driver wax nostalgic for his Haitian punch, Trini chutneys, and Jamaican pumpkin fritters. These conversations whet my kids' appetites for what I hope will be many, many years of travels that yield countless and immeasurable rewards. Luckily for all of us, our neighborhoods have grown rich with residents that hail from points south, and with them has come accessibility to many of the tropical fruits, vegetables, and herbs previously enjoyed only through long journeys. Now, thankfully, it's easy to re-create treats that one previously had to travel far to enjoy.

Though these easy-to-follow recipes present only a tiny sampling of what this part of the world has to offer, they will give you the chance to begin a new chapter in cocktail and appetizer discovery, or perhaps continue a voyage already begun, or even provide a welcome reunion with tastes you had left behind. Like its predecessor, *Mambo Mixers*, this collection of 50 cocktails and 20 appetizers is designed to be accessible to all, from the home cook to the experienced chef. Complete with pairing and serving suggestions, *Calypso Coolers* will guide you into creating a party paradise, no matter what the occasion or season, and fill you with inspiration and energy matched only by the delight a visit to one of the numerous embracing coasts of the Caribbean can deliver. Open this book, bring the journey into your home, and enjoy!

Longevity—and a broad and growing following—can propel a cocktail into the realm of classics. Find out why the drinks in this section have sated so many thirsty fans!

CLASSIC CARIBBEAN COCKTAILS

13   Belize Cocktail

14   *Tostones*

15   El Presidente

16   Blue Mountain Cocktail

17   Dark & Stormy

18   Bahama Mama

19   Rum Shrub

20   Dominican Hurricane

22   Juanita's Yuca Fritters

24   Rum Sour

25   Brown Cow

26   Spanish Town Cocktail

Belize Cocktail and *Tostones* (page 14)

Belize Cocktail

I first heard about this cocktail on a flight from Miami to New York when I was seated next to a gentleman from Belize. We started chatting, and of course I couldn't resist the opportunity to inquire about his national cocktail. "Our national cocktail," he said, smiling, "is delicious." I was enjoying his richly accented voice as he continued proudly. "The most popular drink in our beautiful country is called the Pantée Rippah." I found the name enchanting and repeated it to myself. My co-passenger grinned boyishly as he suggested, "But perhaps, Miss, you would prefer the Boxer Rippah?" It was then that I suddenly realized my misunderstanding of this cocktail's name! Well, by any name, it's hard to resist this simple combination of coconut rum and pineapple juice.

Serves 1

- 2 ounces coconut rum
- 2 ounces unsweetened pineapple juice
- 1 cup ice cubes
- 1 pineapple wedge or maraschino cherry, for garnish

Combine all of the ingredients—except for the garnish—in a shaker. Pour into a wine or cocktail glass, garnish, and serve.

Tostones

If I hadn't known that these toasted plantains were a favorite in the Dominican Republic, a recent trip certainly confirmed it! Whether served with a fabulously cold Presidente (Dominican beer) in the Plaza de Colón in Santo Domingo, or as a side dish with just about any meal, tostones *are clearly important to* los Dominicanos. *And why wouldn't they be? They're certainly* deliciosos. *With the same addictive quality as potato chips, these twice-fried treats marry well with any cocktail. Some serve their* tostones *with ketchup or with* mojito, *a traditional garlic dipping sauce; I prefer them with a squeeze of fresh lime.*

See photo on page 12

Makes about 24 *tostones*

  4 green or slightly yellow plantains
     Canola oil, for frying
     Salt
     Fresh lime slices, for serving-platter garnish

Peel the plantains by running them under warm water, cutting a lengthwise slit down each, and pulling the skin back. Cut into 1-inch-thick slices.

Heat the canola oil in a heavy pan and fry the plantains, without crowding, until golden-brown (about 2 to 3 minutes on each side). Remove from the oil using a slotted spoon or tongs (don't discard the oil!) and drain on paper towels.

Flatten the plantains using the bottom of a flat-bottomed glass bottle, a heavy pan, or a spatula. Heat the reserved oil and fry the flattened plantains again for 30 seconds on each side. Salt as desired and serve immediately with fresh lime slices.

El Presidente

This cocktail, named for early-nineteenth-century Cuban President Mario García Menocal, has numerous variations. This one, apparently not too dissimilar from its namesake, is light and breezy, but somewhat sneaky! Serve with Tostones *(page 14), or Toasted Garbanzo Beans (page 30).*

Serves 1

> Ice cubes
> 1 ½ ounces light rum
> ½ ounce dry vermouth
> ½ ounce Cointreau
> ½ ounce fresh lemon juice, plus 1 thin lemon rind strip, for garnish
> Dash grenadine

In a shaker filled with ice cubes, combine the light rum, dry vermouth, Cointreau, lemon juice, and grenadine. Shake well and stir into a chilled martini glass. Garnish with lemon rind and serve.

Blue Mountain Cocktail

Jamaica's Blue Mountains are not only beautiful, they're also known for producing some of the best coffee in the world. Coffee was brought to Jamaica from Hispaniola in the early part of the eighteenth century, and in the 1800s the island became the world's leading coffee producer. Though coffee production in Jamaica has greatly declined since then, a number of local farmers still cultivate and roast their beans—according to their own special recipes. This cocktail, which boasts Tía María, Jamaica's coffee liqueur, and fresh citrus juices, really packs a punch! Serve with Jamaican Banana Fritters (page 36) or Black-Eyed Pea Fritters (page 92).

Serves 1

Ice cubes

1 ounce fresh orange juice

½ ounce fresh lemon or lime juice, plus 1 thin rind strip for garnish

1½ ounces golden or white rum

½ ounce vodka

½ ounce Tía María (or your favorite coffee liqueur)

Combine all of the ingredients in an ice-filled shaker and shake well. Pour into a tall glass, garnish, and serve.

Dark & Stormy

If you were to inquire, Bermudians would most likely point out that their beloved country is not in the Caribbean at all, but in the Atlantic. After all, these beautiful islands are set about 900 miles east of North Carolina. Still, Bermuda has the color, flavor, and feel of a Caribbean island—which is why this cocktail is included here! I learned about it in New York, where my neighbors Bob and Valerie Rendon, devoted fans of this drink and its birthplace, will tell you that there are no possible substitutions for the Goslings Black Seal rum combined with ginger beer in this recipe. Serve with Tostones *(page 14) or* Puerto Rican Corn Sticks *(page 84).*

Serves 1

- ½ lime, plus 1 half-moon lime slice, for garnish
  Ice cubes
- 2 ounces Goslings Black Seal rum
- 4 ounces Ginger Beer (see page 48, or buy some at a market that carries West Indian products)

Squeeze the lime over a glass filled with ice. Add the rum, followed by the ginger beer. Stir just to blend, garnish, and serve.

Bahama Mama

Perhaps it was the rich, inviting, French-accented voice and hip-moving music of multitalented (and multilingual) André Toussaint (whose song "Little Nassau Bahama Mama" is great background music for this cocktail of the same name!) that inspired this drink in the first place. Whatever the case, this cocktail can be found—with a number of variations—throughout the Caribbean and beyond. Serve with Pumpkin Fritters (page 106), Costa Rican–Style Corn Cakes (page 62), or Tostones (page 14).

Serves 2

1   ounce coconut rum

2   ounces dark rum

1   ounce coffee liqueur

8   ounces unsweetened pineapple juice

1   ounce fresh lemon juice

1   cup ice cubes

2   pineapple wedges, for garnish

Combine all of the ingredients, except the pineapple wedges, in a cocktail shaker with ice. Shake and pour into two cocktail glasses. Garnish and serve.

Rum Shrub

The shrub is a drink made from fruit (in this case citrus peels) steeped in liquor for at least one week. When you're peeling your oranges, try to get as little of the pith as possible, to keep the flavor from being too bitter. Serve with Toasted Garbanzo Beans (page 30) or any of your favorite appetizers.

Makes 1 quart (32 ounces) of fruit-steeped rum, enough to make between 10 and 16 drinks

- 4 oranges, plus about 20 half-moon slices, for garnish
- 1/2 cup turbinado sugar
- 4 ounces water
- 32 ounces dark rum
- Splash of club soda

Cut the skins off the oranges, then cut them into 1/4-inch-thick pieces (so that you can press them easily into a bottle of rum).

In a medium saucepan, bring the sugar and water to a boil and simmer for several minutes, until the sugar is completely dissolved. Let the syrup cool.

Pour the syrup and orange rinds into a rum bottle. (You may have to make room; simply prepare a couple of rum cocktails so that you have to remove some of the liquid from the bottle!) Close the bottle and let steep for at least one week (and up to six). When ready to serve, pour 2 to 3 ounces over ice. Add a splash of club soda, garnish with orange slices, and serve.

Dominican Hurricane

Though we've seen a lot of drinks travel from the Caribbean to points north,
this cocktail took the opposite route! Legend has it that it was originally invented
in the 1940s by Pat O'Brien in New Orleans. Though it seems that no one's sure
when it traveled to the Dominican Republic, where I first enjoyed a version fifteen
years ago in a bar that used to sit across from Diego Columbus's (Christopher's
son's) house, this cousin of the daiquiri deliciously combines elements that
are found throughout the region. Try this with Juanita's Yuca Fritters (page 22),
Sweet Plantains Wrapped in Bacon (page 96), or Tostones (page 14).

Serves 1

- 2 ounces gold or white rum
- 1 ounce passion fruit nectar
- 1 ounce unsweetened pineapple juice
- 1 ounce fresh orange juice
- 1 teaspoon superfine sugar, or to taste
- 1/2 ounce fresh lime juice, plus 1 thin rind strip for garnish
- Dash Angostura bitters
- 1 cup ice cubes

Combine all of the ingredients, except for the orange slice, in a cocktail shaker and shake well. Pour into a glass, garnish, and serve.

Dominican Hurricane and Juanita's Yuca Fritters (page 22)

Juanita's Yuca Fritters

Juanita is the quintessential Dominican mom and grandma: She's got a smile (not to mention the dimples!) that would make anyone swoon, and smooth, rich, café-colored skin, and a tenderness that makes you just want to be around her. She's also an incredible cook, whose philosophy is "del mar al caldero," from the sea to the pot. Everything she makes is fresh—and fabulous.

This recipe is a version of her yuca arepitas, or fritters (though I've replaced the fresh-grated yuca she uses with more manageable soft-cooked yuca flesh— ideally fresh, but frozen is fine, too), gently sweetened with sugar and milk and lightly kissed with the exotic flavor of anise. As an appetizer (great alongside Jamaican Jerk Chicken, page 78) or even as a side dish, this treat marries well with just about any cocktail. Prepare the fritters before guests arrive and serve immediately, or reheat them in a 400°F oven for about 10 minutes.

See photo on page 21

Makes about 25 fritters

1 (24-ounce) bag frozen yuca, cooked; or 2 pounds peeled and coarsely chopped fresh yuca (cut into 3-inch sections with a sharp knife), cooked in salted boiling water for 20 to 30 minutes (or until tender), drained well, core strings removed, and mashed with a potato masher

1 tablespoon turbinado sugar

½ teaspoon Kosher or large-grain sea salt

1 tablespoon unsalted butter, softened

3 tablespoons milk

3 pinches aniseed

1 teaspoon baking soda

Canola oil, for frying

Mango Chutney (page 64; optional)

Place the mashed yuca in a large bowl. Add the sugar, salt, butter, and milk. Mix well, using a potato masher or spoon. Stir in the aniseed and baking soda. When cool enough to handle, divide the dough into 1-inch-wide (and about ¼-inch-thick) pancakes. (At this point you have the option to cover the fritters and set them aside to fry later.)

Heat about 1 inch of oil in a heavy frying pan. Fry the fritters, a few at a time to avoid crowding, for 3 to 5 minutes, or until golden. As they're frying, use a fork to poke small holes in them; this will hasten the frying process and also make them cook more evenly. Let drain on paper towels. Serve immediately by themselves, or with little bowls of Mango Chutney (page 64) for spooning on top.

Rum Sour

On a recent trip to the Dominican Republic, I couldn't help but notice that rum sours appeared on the cocktail menus of many bars in the capital. Served in thick glasses wrapped with thin white paper blankets (to avoid slippage!), these light and fresh cocktails are the perfect companion to Juanita's Yuca Fritters (page 22), Pumpkin Fritters (page 106), Tostones (page 14) and pretty much anything else. Sours, which have been sating the thirsty for some 150 years, can be made with a variety of spirits. The constant, however, is the citrus (fresh lemon or lime juice), as well as a bit of sugar. (Personally I prefer fresh lime juice, but lemon is fine as well.) For its cousin, the Collins, top off with a bit of club soda.

Serves 1

    Ice cubes

2 ounces light rum

1 ounce fresh lime or lemon juice, plus 1 half-moon citrus slice, for garnish

1 teaspoon superfine sugar, or to taste

In a shaker filled with ice cubes, combine the rum, lime juice, and sugar. Shake well and stir into a chilled martini glass. Garnish and serve.

Brown Cow

If you're a coffee-with-milk fan, you'll love this classic cocktail! I like serving this Jamaican-born drink toward the end of sultry summer evening barbecues (maybe because it seems like a dessert). Simple, tasty, and refreshing, this combination goes beautifully with Juanita's Yuca Fritters (page 22) and Pumpkin Fritters (page 106).

Serves 1

- 4 ounces Tía María (or your favorite coffee liqueur)
- 4 ounces milk
- 1 cup ice cubes
  Ground nutmeg, for garnish

Combine all of the ingredients, except the nutmeg, in a shaker. Shake vigorously, pour into a glass, and serve. Garnish with ground nutmeg.

Spanish Town Cocktail

Named after the former capital of beautiful Jamaica, this drink has gained popularity way beyond that island's borders. In fact, there's a very similar cocktail called "Stuyvesant Cooler," apparently named after the Dutch-born seventeenth-century notoriously hot-tempered governor of New Amsterdam— who also served in the West Indies—Peter Stuyvesant. This light and refreshing libation goes quite well with Salmon Patties (page 42) or Codfish Cakes (page 74), accompanied by Carrot & Raisin Salad (page 67).

Serves 1

- 2 ounces light rum
- ½ ounce Cointreau, triple sec, or clear Curaçao
- 1 cup ice cubes
- 1 half-moon orange slice, for garnish

Combine all of the ingredients, except the orange slice. Strain into a chilled martini glass. Garnish and serve.

This collection of sunny, fruit-filled drinks, and the accompanying snacks, complement any summer day—and can gently usher that season right into your arms (and palate!) during the fiercest of winter storms.

DAIQUIRIS & TROPICAL-INFUSED COCKTAILS

28 Banana Daiquiri

30 Toasted Garbanzo Beans

31 Papaya Daiquiri

32 Orange Daiquiri

33 Frozen Daiquiri

35 Guava Daiquiri

36 Jamaican Banana Fritters

37 Ginger Lemonade

38 Costa Rican
Green Plantain Appetizer

40 Ginger-Champagne Cocktail

42 Salmon Patties

45 Mandarin Orange Cocktail

46 Okra Polenta

48 Ginger Beer

49 Jamaican Beer Cooler

50 Virgin Island Cooler

Banana Daiquiri

The banana has contributed to the Caribbean's vital fruit-export industry for years. This fruit made its first appearance in the Dominican Republic in the 1500s, thanks to Portuguese colonists who brought it to Hispaniola. Soon after, the banana became popular throughout the Caribbean as well as Central America. Today it's easy to find miles of beautiful hands of bananas flourishing under the rich prehistoric-looking leaves of the banana plants. This classic banana, rum, and lime-juice cocktail is the perfect counterbalance to salty Tostones *(page 14)* or Toasted Garbanzo Beans *(page 30).*

Serves 1

4 ounces golden rum

1 ounce Cointreau

Juice of 2 limes (about 1 ounce), plus 2 full-moon lime slices, for garnish

8 inches ripe banana (or about 1 1/2 ripe bananas)

1 to 2 teaspoons superfine sugar, or to taste

1 cup ice cubes

Combine all of the ingredients, except the lime slices, in a blender, and process until smooth. Pour into chilled martini glasses, garnish with lime slices, and serve immediately.

Banana Daiquiri, Papaya Daiquiri (page 31), and Toasted Garbanzo Beans (page 30)

Toasted Garbanzo Beans

Easy, healthy, and tasty, these roasted beans are great because you can prepare them ahead of time or serve them up quickly for an impromptu get-together. Called channa *in Trinidad, this roasted version of the nutlike buttery-flavored bean is great with cocktails or served atop a salad for an extra crunch of flavor. Here they're roasted with chili powder and cumin, but you should try—as they do in Trinidad—to combine them with other spices, such as cayenne or curry.*

See photo on page 29
Serves 4

1 (15.5-ounce) can garbanzo beans (or chickpeas)	1/2 teaspoon chili powder, or to taste
2 tablespoons olive oil	1/2 teaspoon coarse sea salt, or to taste
1/2 teaspoon ground cumin, or to taste	1 lime wedge

Preheat the oven to 450°F. Drain and rinse the garbanzos. Blot them dry with a paper towel.

In a bowl, toss the beans with the olive oil and 1/4 teaspoon each of the cumin, chili powder, and salt. Spread on a baking sheet and bake for about 35 minutes, until toasted and crunchy. Check frequently, using a spatula to move the beans around. As it gets toward the end of the cooking time, watch the beans carefully to avoid burning.

Once they're done, let them cool for about 5 minutes, then transfer them to a small ceramic serving dish (I like using Spanish-style terra-cotta dishes), add the remaining cumin, chili powder, and sea salt, and serve. They can be stored in an airtight container for up to one week. Squeeze the juice from the lime wedge on top of the beans just before serving.

Papaya Daiquiri

As one New York fruit vendor said to me recently, "Ripeness of a papaya is a touch thing." Softness is clearly the key to whether your papaya is ripe; it should be tender to the touch. When you do find a ripe papaya, try making this tasty cocktail, which goes really well with Puerto Rican Corn Sticks (page 84) or Caribbean Guacamole (page 56).

See photo on page 29
Serves 1

- 2   ounces light rum
- 1   ounce fresh lime juice, plus 1 full-moon lime slice, for garnish
- 1   teaspoon superfine sugar, or to taste
- $3/4$ cup diced ripe papaya
- $1/2$ cup ice cubes

Combine all of the ingredients, except for the lime slice, in a blender, and process until smooth. Pour into a chilled wine glass, garnish with the lime slice, and serve immediately.

Orange Daiquiri

Oranges have been flourishing in the Caribbean since they were brought to the region (supposedly by Christopher Columbus) in the latter part of the fifteenth century. Whether in liqueurs, sauces, grilled dishes, or on their own, fresh orange juice is for many of us northerners synonymous with sunshine. This summery cocktail is a nice match with Sweet Plantains Wrapped in Bacon (page 96).

Serves 1

- 2 ounces light rum
- 1 tablespoon Curaçao, Cointreau, or Grand Marnier
- 2 tablespoons fresh orange juice, plus 1 half-moon orange slice, for garnish
- 2 tablespoons fresh lime juice
- 1/2 cup ice cubes

Combine all the ingredients, except for the lime slice, in a blender. Pour into a cocktail glass, garnish, and serve.

Frozen Daiquiri

Born in Cuba, the daiquiri has won the hearts of rum and lime lovers around the globe. This slushy version is perfect on steamy summer afternoons. You can easily double this recipe, make batches, and keep them ready to go in the freezer (just mix well and garnish before serving). Serve with Jamaican Jerk Chicken (page 78) or any of your favorite appetizers.

Serves 4

- 8 ounces light rum
- 8 ounces fresh lime juice, plus 4 half-moon lime slices, for garnish
- 4 ounces Cointreau
- 4 teaspoons superfine sugar, or to taste
- 2 cups ice cubes

Combine all of the ingredients, except for the lime slice, in a blender and process until smooth. Pour into chilled wine glasses, garnish with the lime slices, and serve immediately.

Guava Daiquiri and Jamaican Banana Fritters (page 36)

Guava Daiquiri

The soft, pink flesh of a fresh guava exudes a perfume and flavor that is intoxicating. This tropical fruit, found flourishing along roadsides in the Dominican Republic and Puerto Rico—and in several varieties (and shades) on many other islands—yields a luscious nectar that combines beautifully with fresh lime juice and, of course, rum. Though fresh guavas may be hard to come by in areas north of the Caribbean, excellent-quality nectar is not. Enjoy guava daiquiris with Jamaican Banana Fritters (page 36), Puerto Rican Corn Sticks (page 84), and Jamaican Jerk Chicken (page 78).

Serves 1

    Ice cubes
 2 ounces light or golden rum
 3 ounces guava nectar
 1 ounce fresh lime juice, plus 1 full-moon lime slice, for garnish
 ¼ ounce Cointreau

In a shaker filled with ice cubes, combine the rum, guava nectar, lime juice, and Cointreau. Shake well and strain into a chilled martini glass. Place the lime slice in the cocktail. Serve immediately.

Jamaican Banana Fritters

I was about six years old the first time I visited Jamaica, so I don't remember too much—but I do remember these fritters! My parents took all three children (the fourth wasn't born yet!), and we stayed in a house in Ocho Ríos. Not too long after our return—and up until recently—my mother loved to prepare heaping platters of these delicious plantain pancakes, gently sprinkled with confectioners' sugar, to serve as a side dish alongside ham or roast turkey. Today I make them to serve with cocktails, such as the Guava Daiquiri (page 35), and other appetizers, such as Jamaican Jerk Chicken (page 78) and Carrot & Raisin Salad (page 67).

See photo on page 34

Serves about 8

4 ripe bananas, mashed

2 eggs, beaten

1 teaspoon turbinado sugar

1 teaspoon vanilla extract

1 1/2 teaspoons baking powder

1 cup all-purpose flour

1/2 cup raisins

   Canola oil for frying

   Confectioners' or superfine sugar, for dusting

In a medium-size bowl, combine the bananas, eggs, sugar, and vanilla. Stir in the baking powder and flour, and mix until well blended. Stir in the raisins.

Pour enough oil into a frying pan to coat it well. Heat over a medium flame. Drop the batter in by teaspoonfuls and cook for about 2 minutes on each side, or until golden. Drain on paper towels and serve immediately, or keep warm in a moderate oven for about 20 minutes. Dust with sugar just before serving.

Ginger Lemonade

Ginger-brushed cocktails, like this lemonade, are popular throughout the Caribbean, thanks to Eastern influences. (In fact, fresh ginger limeade and lemonade can be found in India and Japan!) This very refreshing vodka-spiked lemonade, a version of that found in Trinidad and other parts of the Caribbean, can be made with or without the alcohol. If you are making it without alcohol, add about half a cup of the lemonade and an equal amount of club soda. You can also use the lemonade for another luscious drink, the Ginger-Champagne Cocktail (page 40). This lemonade makes a great companion to Juanita's Yuca Fritters (page 22).

Serves 4

16 ounces water

2 inches fresh gingerroot, peeled and sliced

1 cup granulated sugar, plus more to taste

6 ounces fresh lemon juice, plus 4 half-moon slices of lemon, for garnish

2 ounces fresh lime juice

8 ounces vodka

Crushed ice

Club soda

Fresh mint leaves and/or sugarcane sticks, for garnish

In a medium saucepan, combine 1 cup of the water with the ginger and sugar, and cook over a medium flame, stirring frequently, until the sugar has dissolved. Let cool to room temperature. Strain into a pitcher. Add the remaining water, lemon juice, and lime juice, and either refrigerate for up to one week, or mix with the vodka for immediate serving.

Fill four glasses with crushed ice. Add 2 ounces of vodka to each glass. Fill three-quarters of the way with the ginger-lemonade mixture. Stir and top with club soda. Garnish and serve.

Costa Rican Green Plantain Appetizer

This dish—called picadillo *in Costa Rica—is quite versatile: It can be an appetizer as suggested here, or an entrée served over steaming white rice. It can also be made with or without the meat, depending on your—and your guests'—preferences. For a cocktail party, serve warm or at room temperature, rolled into warm flour tortillas, or in small dishes with your favorite tortilla chips. You can make this dish ahead of time (adding everything except the cilantro), then heat and add the cilantro just before serving.*

Serves about 8 to 10

- 2 large green plantains, peeled (according to directions on page 14) and each cut into thirds
- 2 teaspoons vegetable oil
- 1 teaspoon unsalted butter
- 1/4 teaspoon ground cumin
- 1/4 teaspoon paprika
- 1/4 cup chopped red onion
- 1/4 cup chopped red bell pepper
- 1/4 cup minced celery
- 1 clove garlic, minced
- 1/2 pound lean ground beef or sausage, removed from casing
- 1 cup diced cherry or grape tomatoes
- Salt and freshly ground black pepper
- Hot sauce
- 1/4 cup fresh chopped cilantro leaves

In a medium saucepan, bring 2 cups of water to a boil. Add the plantains and cook for about 15 minutes, or until the plantains are soft. Drain, reserving the liquid. When the plantains are cool enough to handle, dice them into $\frac{1}{4}$-inch chunks. Reserve the liquid.

Meanwhile, heat oil and butter in a saucepan over medium-high heat. Add cumin, paprika, onion, red pepper, celery, and garlic. Fry them for 3 minutes. Add lean ground beef or sausage and stir well. Cook over low heat for 10 minutes, or until the meat is cooked, stirring constantly and breaking up the larger chunks. Add about $\frac{1}{2}$ cup of the plantain liquid, and more as needed (so that the mixture doesn't dry out). Add the tomatoes, diced plantains, salt, pepper, and hot sauce to taste. Simmer for 5 minutes. Sprinkle with cilantro. Let rest at room temperature for about 20 minutes before serving.

Ginger-Champagne Cocktail

This light and refreshing cocktail is guaranteed to whet your appetite! It's perfect for a Sunday brunch, served alongside Salmon Patties (page 42), Carrot & Raisin Salad (page 67), and/or Caribbean Guacamole (page 56). For more than one serving, simply multiply the amounts.

Serves 1

- 1 ounce Ginger Lemonade (page 37), or to taste
- 1 lime wedge
- 1 lemon wedge
- 5 ounces cold Spanish sparkling wine or dry champagne
  Dash Angostura bitters

Pour the lemonade into a wine glass. Squeeze the lime and lemon wedges, and drop them in. Top with the sparkling wine or champagne. Add the bitters and serve.

Ginger-Champagne Cocktail and Salmon Patties (page 42)

Salmon Patties

Sofia and Wes, my two teenaged kids, eat these so quickly, I have to double the recipe to have enough for guests, too! These golden, red pepper–flecked patties are similar to crabcakes. If you're not serving them immediately, set them aside and then, just prior to serving, place the patties on baking sheets and heat in a 400°F oven until warm, about 10 minutes. Serve them with Ginger-Champagne Cocktails (page 40), or Ginger Lemonade (page 37), with or without the vodka.

See photo on page 41

Makes about 20 small patties

1	(15-ounce) can (or two 7.5-ounce cans) salmon, drained
1	sleeve of a 1-pound box Saltine crackers, crushed
2	eggs, slightly beaten
$\frac{1}{2}$	cup finely chopped onion
$\frac{1}{2}$	cup finely chopped red bell pepper
1	tablespoon fresh lemon juice
1	teaspoon grated lemon zest
$1\frac{1}{2}$	teaspoons minced fresh rosemary, or $\frac{1}{2}$ teaspoon dried and crushed rosemary
$\frac{1}{4}$	teaspoon cayenne pepper, or to taste
	Canola oil for frying
	Lemon or lime wedges

In a large bowl, combine the salmon, crushed crackers, and eggs. Mix well using a wooden spoon or your hands. Add the onion, red bell pepper, lemon juice, lemon zest, rosemary, and cayenne. Shape into 20 patties. (If they're not sticking together, add a few more crushed crackers.)

Heat enough oil in a sauté pan to cover the bottom generously. Cook the patties in hot oil until nicely browned on both sides, about 2 minutes per side. Drain on paper towels and serve on a tray with plenty of lemon and/or lime wedges for both color and flavor.

Mandarin Orange Cocktail and Okra Polenta (page 46)

Mandarin Orange Cocktail

Marinating citrus rinds in rum is a common way of flavoring rums in the Caribbean. This cocktail requires some advance preparation (the orange peels should rest in the rum for about five days before making the drink), but the unique light, summery flavors are worth the wait. Serve with Salmon Patties (page 42), Jamaican Banana Fritters (page 36), or Juanita's Yuca Fritters (page 22).

Serves 4 to 8

- 16 ounces rum
- $\frac{1}{2}$ cup mandarin orange peels (with as little pith as possible)
- 1 cup superfine sugar
- 8 ounces water
- 8 thin strips of orange rind or half-moon orange slices, for garnish
  Ice cubes

In a large glass jar or pitcher, combine the rum and orange peels. Cover and refrigerate for about five days. Strain and remove the orange peels.

Combine the sugar and water in a small saucepan and simmer until the sugar has dissolved and the water has reduced by half. Let chill to room temperature before combining with the strained rum. Chill in the refrigerator for at least an hour. Serve in glasses with ice, garnished with the orange slices.

⊸ Okra Polenta

Okra is a vegetable traditionally associated with southern dishes in the United States, but it has been eaten throughout the Caribbean—and Latin America— for years. Called coo-coo *or* cou-cou *in most of the Caribbean, this African-born dish (I borrowed the name from its Italian cousin!) is a staple on many islands. This is a great dish to serve to introduce people to okra; if possible, use fresh instead of frozen. Though you can use fine or coarse yellow cornmeal, the flavor of the latter has more depth. The comforting flavor and texture of cornmeal offers a nice balance with the okra and corn kernels. Okra Polenta is great with any fruit-based cocktail.*

See photo on page 44
Makes about 16 squares (or triangles)

- 2 cups okra, fresh or frozen
- 2 tablespoons unsalted butter
- 1 small onion, finely diced
- 1/2 teaspoon cayenne pepper
- 48 ounces water or chicken stock
  Kosher salt
- 2 cups yellow cornmeal, preferably coarse
  Freshly ground black pepper
- 1/4 teaspoon freshly ground nutmeg, to taste
- 1 cup cooked corn kernels
- 2 tablespoons minced red bell pepper, for garnish
- 1 tablespoon chopped parsley leaves, for garnish

If using frozen okra, put it into a strainer and run it under cool water for a few minutes to thaw. Remove the stems from the okra and cut them into $1/4$-inch-thick slices. Heat 1 tablespoon of the butter in a skillet over medium-high heat. Cook the onion until it begins to soften. Add the okra and cayenne pepper. Cook for 1 minute and set aside.

Butter a 13x9-inch pan with the remaining tablespoon of butter. Bring the water or stock to a boil in a large saucepan and add 1 teaspoon of salt. Gradually pour in the cornmeal, stirring constantly to avoid lumps. Then stir in the okra and onion. Reduce the heat to low, season with salt, black pepper, and nutmeg, to taste, and cook for about 15 minutes, or until the cornmeal mixture is creamy. Stir in the corn, and pour into the buttered dish, smooth on top with a spatula, and let cool.

Invert the dish onto a large platter, or slice the cooled cornmeal into squares (or triangles) and serve at room temperature. You can also fry the cornmeal squares for a few minutes in butter or olive oil to make them crisp on the outside and soft on the inside. Garnish with peppers and parsley just before serving.

Ginger Beer

It's not too difficult to find ginger beer in the market these days, but making it on your own will give you a newfound appreciation for this drink. It will also help you understand why this refreshing libation—in slightly different interpretations—is so popular throughout the Caribbean. This version is, as my kids point out, like a really delicious ginger ale. It doesn't contain alcohol, unlike some versions. Though it is popular year-round, this drink is traditionally served in the English-speaking islands around Christmastime. Serve with Toasted Garbanzo Beans (page 30) or Tostones *(page 14).*

Serves 1

   1 cup fresh ginger, peeled and thinly sliced
      Juice of one lime or lemon
   3 cloves
  48 ounces water
  ½ cup superfine sugar, or to taste

In a medium saucepan, combine the ginger, lime or lemon juice, cloves, and water. Bring to a boil, then lower the heat to medium. Let simmer for about 5 minutes. Remove from the heat and let stand at least 4 hours or overnight. Strain and sweeten to taste. If the mixture is too strong, add water to taste.

Jamaican Beer Cooler

This Jamaican version of the Mexican michelada *is very refreshing—and quite powerful, thanks to the rum!*

Serves 2

4 ½   ounces white rum
  8   ounces pineapple juice
  1   pint beer, preferably Red Stripe (Jamaican Beer)
  2   cups crushed ice
      Pinch ground nutmeg
      Pinch ground cinnamon
  2   pineapple triangles or half-moon orange slices, for garnish

In a pitcher, combine the rum, pineapple juice, and beer. Stir just to mix. Pour into two chilled glasses filled with crushed ice. Sprinkle with nutmeg and cinnamon, garnish, and serve.

Virgin Island Cooler

Orange flower water is a fragrant concoction used in many baked goods (both savory and sweet) as well as in cocktails. Found primarily in Middle Eastern markets, this welcome flavor adds a wonderful touch to this refreshing cocktail. Serve with Toasted Garbanzo Beans (page 30), Tostones (page 14), or Puerto Rican Corn Sticks (page 84).

Serves 1

- 2 ounces light rum
- 1/2 ounce dark rum
- 1 ounce brandy
- 1 teaspoon turbinado sugar, or to taste
- 2 1/2 ounces fresh orange juice, plus 1 half-moon orange slice, for garnish
- 1 1/2 ounces fresh lemon juice
- Dash orange flower water
- Splash lemon-lime soda
- 1 cup ice cubes

Combine all of the ingredients, except the orange slice, in a shaker and shake briskly. Pour into a tall glass, garnish, and serve.

Just as a child does when playing with a new toy, you'll rejoice as you devour these intensely rewarding flavors! Exciting new taste combinations—like those in this chapter—will treat you to an always-deserved fresh-air break from your routine.

MARTINIS & CARIBBEAN-FRUIT COCKTAILS

53 Coconut Martini

54 Sorrel Martini

55 Pineapple Martini

56 Caribbean Guacamole

57 Mango Martini

58 Gin & Coconut Water

59 Banana Colada

60 Caribbean Cosmopolitan

62 Costa Rican–Style Corn Cakes (*Arepas*)

64 Mango Chutney

65 Passion Fruit Cocktail Caribbean Style

67 Carrot & Raisin Salad

68 Papaya Flower

70 Curaçao Cocktail

Assorted Caribbean Martinis and Tortilla Chips

Coconut Martini

Though rum is clearly the spirit of choice throughout the Caribbean—and rightly so—vodka appears frequently . . . and makes this coconut-infused drink a delightful one. Serve with Salmon Patties (page 42) or the Caribbean-Style Tuna Salad (page 89).

Serves 2

- 1 lime wedge
- 2 tablespoons sweetened coconut flakes
- 4 ounces vodka
- 1 ounce cream of coconut
  Splash unsweetened pineapple juice (optional)
- 1 cup ice cubes

Rub the rims of two chilled martini glasses with the wedge of lime. Pour the coconut flakes onto a plate, and press the rims of the glasses into them, turning gently until the rims are evenly coated. Combine the remaining ingredients in a cocktail shaker. Shake briskly. Strain into glasses and serve.

Sorrel Martini

It's only a matter of time before sorrel, or dried hibiscus flowers, becomes the next big ingredient north of the Caribbean. (I've already seen sorrel caipirinhas, coladas, and even martinis in the New York area!) As healthy as it is colorful, sorrel is slowly working its way—thanks to the Caribbean and Latin American communities—into the mainstream of northern neighbors' drinks and cocktails. Serve with Jamaican Jerk Chicken (page 78), Tostones (page 14), and/or Salmon Patties (page 42).

Serves 2

1 ½ cups dried sorrel blossoms, found in Caribbean or Latin markets
       (it's called *flor de Jamaica*—pronounced hah-MY-kah—
       or *rosa de Jamaica*), picked over, discolored pieces discarded
  4 ounces vodka
  1 ounce Cointreau or triple sec
  1 cup ice cubes
  2 strips lemon rind, for garnish

Combine all of the ingredients, except for the lemon rinds, in a shaker. Shake vigorously, strain into two chilled martini glasses, and garnish.

Pineapple Martini

This martini is great for vodka and pineapple lovers! Unlike some other fruits we find at the market, the pineapple needs to be picked ripe. So when you're choosing pineapples, look for fresh ones with deep-green leaves that show no dryness (yellowing or browning). Ripe pineapples should give off a good, fresh, tropical smell. Serve these martinis with Panamanian Ceviche (Page 99), Costa Rican–Style Corn Cakes (page 62), or Jamaican Jerk Chicken (page 78).

See photo on page 52
Serves 1

- ¼ cup fresh pineapple, plus additional wedge, for garnish
- 2 ounces vodka
   Ice cubes
   Splash unsweetened pineapple juice

Pour the fresh pineapple chunks into a tall shaker. Add the vodka. Use a pestle or the end of a wooden spoon to muddle (mash together) the pineapple pieces and vodka. Add the ice, and shake briskly for about a minute. Strain into a chilled martini glass, add the splash of pineapple juice, garnish, and serve.

Caribbean Guacamole

First cultivated in the Caribbean in Jamaica in the seventeenth century, the avocado has since made its way around the region. Of course, guacamole originally hails from Mexico, but this papaya-packed version is sure to win over new fans. Like so many sauces and dips from that part of the world, it has bite—which is only somewhat balanced by the cooling effects of the papaya and cucumber. What you might want to do for parties is make one spiced-up batch for your "hot" fans, and a more mellow one for those who prefer less heat (but be sure you label them!). Try to make your guacamole as close to serving time as possible. Serve with the Papaya Daiquiri (page 31), or your favorite cocktail, along with crispy-fresh tortilla chips.

Makes about 3 cups

- 3 avocados, peeled, seeded, and diced
- 1 papaya, peeled, seeded, and diced
- 2 limes, cut in half
- 1 large or two smaller cucumbers, peeled, seeded, and diced
- 1 jalapeño, Scotch bonnet, or habanero pepper, minced (optional)
- 1/4 teaspoon cayenne pepper (optional)
- Kosher salt and freshly ground black pepper
- 1/4 cup shredded unsweetened coconut

In a large bowl, combine the avocado and papaya. Squeeze the limes over the fruit and toss gently. Add the cucumber. Carefully (so as not to mush the papaya and avocado) stir in the jalapeño and the cayenne pepper. Add salt and pepper to taste. Top with the coconut and serve immediately with your favorite chips.

Mango Martini

Mango mixes beautifully with everything it meets. Tasty, light, and clean, this martini can be served with any of your favorite appetizers. Try it with Salmon Patties (page 42), Caribbean-Style Tuna Salad (page 89), or Sweet Plantains in Bacon (page 96).

Serves 1

> Ice cubes
>
> 2 ounces vodka
>
> 1 ounce fresh mango pulp or mango nectar
>
> ½ ounce fresh lime juice, plus a half-moon lime slice, for garnish

In a tall shaker filled with ice, combine all of the ingredients, except the lime slice. Shake briskly. Strain into a chilled martini glass, garnish, and serve.

Gin & Coconut Water

Just like the song of the same name, this cocktail will get you moving! Ideally, this should be made with fresh coconut water, but if that's not possible, you can find it canned in many West Indian or Latin American markets. Though some versions of this drink include a spoonful of sweetened condensed milk, I prefer it this way (but certainly suggest trying both). Serve with Toasted Garbanzo Beans (page 30) or Costa Rican–Style Corn Cakes (page 62), topped with Mango Chutney (page 64).

Serves 1

- 2 ounces gin
- 6 ounces coconut water
- 1 cup ice cubes

Combine all of the ingredients in a large shaker. Shake briskly and pour into a tall glass.

Banana Colada

Rumor has it that the first piña colada was created at the Caribe Hilton in Puerto Rico—which is actually where I had my first, many moons ago! Since then, there have been many different interpretations using different tropical fruits. This very refreshing version is often made with banana liqueur, but I prefer to use an excellent-quality banana nectar and go heavier on the rum.

Serves 2

- 1 lime wedge
- 1/4 cup shredded sweetened coconut
- 2 ripe bananas, peeled and quartered
- 4 ounces unsweetened pineapple juice
- 4 ounces banana nectar
- 2 ounces cream of coconut
- 4 ounces light or golden rum
- 2 cups ice cubes

Rub the rims of two chilled wine or margarita glasses with the wedge of lime. Pour the coconut flakes onto a plate, and press the rims of the glasses into the flakes, turning gently until the rims are evenly coated.

Combine the bananas, pineapple juice, and banana nectar in a blender. Process until smooth. Add the cream of coconut, rum, and ice, and mix until frothy. Serve immediately.

Caribbean Cosmopolitan

There are many versions of this regional cosmopolitan; this one is a favorite!

Serves 1

   Ice cubes
2 ounces coconut rum
1 ounce Cointreau
½ ounce fresh-squeezed lime juice
   Splash cranberry or cran-raspberry juice
1 thin-sliced lime rind or lemon twist, for garnish

In a tall shaker filled with ice, combine all of the ingredients, except the lime rind or lemon twist. Strain into a chilled martini glass, garnish, and serve.

Caribbean Cosmopolitan, and Costa Rican–Style Corn Cakes (page 62) with Mango Chutney (page 64)

Costa Rican–Style Corn Cakes (Arepas)

"I'll introduce her to my aunt, the best cook I know!" promised Danny when my friend called him in Limón from San José, Costa Rica. When my bus arrived in the port city of the Caribbean province—after a gorgeous roam through lush, jungle-like countryside—I knew I had left the country's busy capital and ventured to a place that was culturally quite different. The soft, rainy breezes (I arrived in rainy season!) brought with them the smell of coconut and the rhythm of reggae. Los limoneses, who are primarily of Afro-Caribbean decent, speak Spanish flecked with English (which at first I thought they were using for my benefit, until I heard absolutely everyone say, "rice and beans!"). Danny and his dad (a dead ringer for Morgan Freeman) introduced me to Aunt Ester, who graciously spent an afternoon telling stories sharing recipes with me. This is a variation of one in her collection. Serve these tasty arepas by themselves or with a small spoonful of Mango Chutney (page 64), along with Mango Sangría (page 82).

See photo on page 61

Makes about 35 small corn cakes

1½ cups instant precooked white (or yellow) cornmeal (*harina precocida* in Spanish)
  1 cup coconut milk (preferably light), at room temperature
  2 teaspoons cream of coconut
  ½ cup chicken broth or hot water (if you use water, add salt to taste)
  ½ cup sweetened or unsweetened coconut flakes (optional)
     Butter, for frying

Pour the cornmeal into a large bowl and add the coconut milk and cream of coconut. Mix well with a fork or wooden spoon. While stirring, gradually pour in the hot chicken broth (or water and salt). Stir in the coconut flakes and mix, using your hands. Cover and let sit for 5 minutes, or you can refrigerate the dough and keep it for up to 1 day.

When you're ready to make the *arepas*, scoop up a heaping teaspoon full of dough and form a small pancake (about 1 $\frac{1}{2}$ inches wide) in the palm of your hand. Repeat with the remaining dough and set the pancakes aside on a platter.

Lightly butter a griddle or heavy skillet. Cook the *arepas* about 3 to 4 minutes on each side, or until golden. (You may need to wipe out the frying pan with a paper towel after a few batches so that the butter doesn't blacken.) Serve immediately. Leftovers, if you have any, can be heated in a toaster (they're great with a bit of butter on top). You can also reheat them in the microwave for 15 seconds and enjoy them as a late-night snack with a glass of wine or port—or even a cup of tea.

Mango Chutney

Chutneys tell the story of migration to the Caribbean. Originally from India, these relishes have evolved as they traveled. Like India, the Caribbean boasts a treasure chest of fruits and vegetables from which these relishes can be made, though the mango and papaya chutneys are probably the most popular. Once you taste this mango chutney, you will be inspired to use it whenever you can! For starters, try it on top of the Costa Rican–Style Corn Cakes (page 62).

See photo on page 61
Makes about 2 cups

- 2 mangoes, peeled and diced
- 1 hot chile peppers (like Scotch bonnet, habanero, or jalapeño), seeded and minced
- ½ cup apple cider vinegar
- 1 tablespoon salt
- 1 teaspoon ground allspice
- 1 tablespoon curry powder
- 2 tablespoons dark brown sugar
- 1 small onion, finely chopped
- ½ cup golden raisins
- 2 tablespoons minced fresh ginger
- Juice of 2 limes
- ½ cup mango nectar

Combine all of the ingredients in an enamel pot and bring to a boil. Reduce the heat to medium and simmer until thickened, about 25 minutes. Remove from the heat, cover, and set aside to cool. Serve immediately or cover and refrigerate, but bring to room temperature prior to serving. The chutney will keep for up to two weeks.

Passion Fruit Cocktail Caribbean Style

Nutmeg, a spice said to have been brought to Grenada (where it's currently cultivated) and Trinidad by British sailors in the 1800s, is a nice touch to a variety of regional foods and drinks. Just a light sprinkle adds a welcome aroma and flavor to this cocktail. Serve with Puerto Rican Corn Sticks (page 84) and Carrot & Raisin Salad (page 67).

See photo on page 66
Serves 2

- 3 ounces passion fruit nectar
- 3 ounces rum
- 1 teaspoon superfine sugar, or to taste
- 1 cup crushed ice
  Dash Angostura bitters
  Freshly grated nutmeg

In a glass shaker, combine the passion fruit nectar, rum, sugar, and ice. Shake well. Pour into chilled wine or cocktail glasses. Add the bitters. Top with a sprinkle of nutmeg and serve.

Passion Fruit Cocktail Caribbean Style (page 65) and Carrot & Raisin Salad

Carrot & Raisin Salad

This salad offers a nice balance to the Puerto Rican Corn Sticks (page 84)—and any fried or spicy dish. It's perfect anytime (and could be a meal in and of itself!), but it is especially cooling on a sticky summer day. Serve in small ramekins with tiny forks, or set a large bowl aside and let your guests help themselves. I recommend—as always—that you use the freshest carrots you can get; it will make the salad that much tastier. Though you can serve this salad with just about any cocktail, it combines particularly well with Passion Fruit Cocktail Caribbean Style (page 65).

Makes about 6 cups of salad

- 5 cups shredded carrots
- 1 cup golden raisins
- 1 1/2 teaspoons minced fresh ginger
- 2 ounces fresh lime juice
- 4 ounces fresh orange juice
- 1/2 cup mayonnaise
- 1 1/2 teaspoons ground cinnamon, plus additional to sprinkle on top
- 1/4 teaspoon ground nutmeg
- Kosher salt and freshly ground black pepper to taste

Combine the carrots, raisins, and ginger in a large mixing bowl. Pour the citrus juices on top. Stir in the mayonnaise, cinnamon, and nutmeg. Add salt and pepper and mix well. Cover and chill in the refrigerator for at least an hour and up to a day. Sprinkle some cinnamon on top just before serving.

Papaya Flower

Papayas, also called pawpaws and tree melons, are a Caribbean favorite. Delightfully sweet with musky undertones, they blend nicely with tangy lime and soft coconut rum in this Costa Rican-inspired drink.

Serves 2

- 1   lime wedge
- 1   teaspoon granulated sugar, plus more to taste
- 1   ounce fresh lime juice, or to taste
- 2   ounces white rum
- 1   ounce coconut rum
- ¾   cup chopped papaya
- 1   cup ice cubes
- 2   pieces star fruit, for garnish

Rub the rims of two chilled margarita or cocktail glasses with the wedge of lime. Pour a teaspoon of granulated sugar onto a plate, and press the rims of the glasses into it, turning gently until the rims are evenly coated. Shake off excess.

Combine the remaining ingredients, except for the star fruit, in a blender. Process until smooth. Taste and add sugar as desired. Pour into the prepared glasses. Garnish with the star fruit and serve.

Papaya Flower

Curaçao Cocktail

Located just 38 miles north of Venezuela, the Caribbean island of Curaçao is the birthplace of the liqueur of the same name. Originally made with the aromatic peels of the bitter orange native to that area, the laraha, *Curaçao adds a flavor not unlike those of Cointreau and triple sec. Serve this cocktail with* Tostones *(page 14) or Puerto Rican Corn Sticks (page 84).*

Serves 2

- 1 ounce grenadine
- 2 tablespoons turbinado sugar, or to taste
- 8 ounces mango nectar
- 3 ounces white rum
- 3 ounces Curaçao
- 1 ounce fresh lime juice
- 1½ cups crushed ice

Pour the grenadine into a shot glass. Dip a finger into the grenadine and then run along the rim of two wine glasses. Pour 1 tablespoon of the sugar onto a plate, and press the rims of the glasses into it, turning gently until the rims are evenly coated.

In a shaker, combine the grenadine, mango nectar, white rum, Curaçao, and lime juice with the ice, and shake briskly. Taste and add sugar as needed. Pour into the glasses and serve.

Punches mean parties! Not literally, of course, but they're a great solution to serving a crowd of thirsty friends. Have fun trying these recipes—and finding your own favorites.

PUNCHES

73   Sorrel Champagne Cocktail

74   Godfish Cakes

76   Dominica Lime Punch

78   Jamaican Jerk Chicken

80   Cucumber Raita with Coconut

81   Jamaican Sorrel Punch

82   Mango Sangría

84   Puerto Rican Corn Sticks

87   Planter's Punch

88   Caribbean Citrus–Rum Champagne Punch

89   Caribbean-Style Tuna Salad

91   Bajan Punch

92   Black-Eyed Pea Fritters

94   Caribe Cocktail Punch

96   Sweet Plantains Wrapped in Bacon

97   Panamanian Papaya Punch

99   Panamanian Ceviche

100   Anguilla Fruit Punch

Sorrel Champagne Cocktail and Codfish Cakes (page 74)

Sorrel Champagne Cocktail

Sorrel is typically considered a Caribbean Christmas drink; combining it with champagne, as is done in Panama and other Caribbean areas, makes it quite festive! It's easy to prepare the sorrel ahead of time, and then pour into a pitcher, with sparkling wine, at the last minute. Try this cocktail with Salmon Patties (page 42), Panamanian Ceviche (page 99), or Codfish Cakes (page 74).

Serves 8 to 12

- 32 ounces water
- 1 cup dried sorrel blossoms, picked over, discolored pieces discarded
- 1 tablespoon grated fresh ginger
- 2 cinnamon sticks
- 3 whole cloves
- 1/2 cup superfine sugar, or to taste
- 1 (750-milliliter) bottle Spanish Cava, Prosecco, or other sparkling wine
  Half-moon orange slices, for garnish

Bring the water to a boil in a large pot. Add the sorrel, ginger, cinnamon sticks, and cloves, and stir. Turn off the heat, cover, and steep for 4 hours or until cooled to room temperature; refrigerate overnight. Strain, sweeten with sugar to taste, and chill well for up to one week. Just before serving, combine the sorrel mixture in equal parts with the sparkling wine. Serve in champagne glasses, garnished with orange slices.

Codfish Cakes

Codfish, one of the most eaten fish in the world, has a great presence in the Caribbean. Whether it's in the Jamaican Stamp and Go or the Puerto Rican bacalaítos, codfish, also called saltfish, is certainly a popular part of many Caribbean diets. These go well with any fruit-based cocktail, but I especially like them with Guava Daiquiris (page 35).

See photo on page 72
Makes about 24 fritters

- 1/2 pound dred and salted codfish, deboned
- 1/2 cup finely chopped scallions
- 1/4 cup finely chopped fresh cilantro leaves, plus additional, for garnish
- 1/2 red bell pepper, finely diced, plus additional, for garnish
- 1/2 Scotch bonnet, jalapeño, or other hot pepper, minced
- 2 cups all-purpose flour
- 2 teaspoons baking powder
- 8 ounces water
  - Salt and freshly ground black pepper, to taste
  - Canola oil, for frying
  - Fresh lime wedges, for platter garnish

Rinse the codfish several times in water. Then place codfish in a medium bowl. Cover it with cold water and let it soak in the refrigerator overnight. Drain well and rinse again (this is to get rid of the excess salt). Place in a saucepan, cover with water, and bring to a boil. Cook for about 15 minutes. Drain, remove any remaining skin and bones. Shred the fish, using the tines of a fork or your fingers.

Place the shredded codfish in a large bowl, and add the scallions, cilantro, and peppers. Mix well. Stir in the flour and baking powder and mix with your hands. Add salt and pepper. Make a little well in the center of the mixture and pour in the water, a little at a time. Mix well, cover, and let sit in the refrigerator for about 10 minutes.

Heat two inches oil in a heavy pan or in a deep fryer set to 365°F. Drop large spoonfuls of the batter into the oil, making sure not to crowd them. Fry for about 2 to 3 minutes on each side, or until golden-brown on both sides. Drain on paper towels, garnish with cilantro and red peppers, and serve.

Dominica Lime Punch

Maybe it's the nutmeg, the citrus-fruit rinds, or the bitters—or the magical blending of all these flavors—that makes this punch so enchanting. Try serving this on a cold winter's day and you'll see how quickly you can change the mood from chilly to tropical! Serve with Jamaican Jerk Chicken (page 78) or Puerto Rican Corn Sticks (page 84).

Serves 10 to 12

12	ounces dark rum
	Rind from 1 lime
1	cup turbinado sugar
16	ounces water
	Rind from 1 orange
	Rind from 1 lemon
$\frac{1}{2}$	teaspoon Angostura bitters
4	ounces fresh lime juice, plus 12–24 full-moon lime slices, for garnish
$\frac{1}{4}$	teaspoon ground nutmeg

Combine the rum and half the lime rind in a glass container. Soak for at least an hour and up to a day before removing the rind.

Meanwhile, in a medium saucepan, combine the sugar and water. Bring to a boil, then lower the heat. Add the remaining lime rind, along with the other rinds. Simmer, stirring frequently, for about 7 minutes. Remove from the heat and let cool to room temperature.

Once the sugar water has cooled, strain it and combine it with the rum, bitters, lime juice, and nutmeg. Pour over ice-filled glasses, garnish, and serve.

Jamaican Jerk Chicken (page 78), Cucumber Raita with Coconut (page 80), and Dominica Lime Punch

Jamaican Jerk Chicken

I urge you to try this not-too-difficult and incredibly tasty (though potentially quite spicy hot) recipe. Not only will it make your home smell terrific, it has such depth—not unlike a Mexican mole sauce—I'm sure your family and friends will be asking you to make it again and again. Jerk recipes vary, but the three main ingredients are chile pepper, allspice, and thyme. If you you're a fan of fire, definitely add the habanero or Scotch bonnet pepper, but here I've made that extra heat optional. You can make these ahead of time, and reheat them, covered in a 400°F oven for about 7 minutes, before your guests arrive. Serve this appetizer with Dominica Lime Punch (page 76), Ginger Lemonade (page 37), Passion Fruit Cocktail Caribbean Style (page 65), or ice-cold Red Stripe (Jamaican) beer.

See photo on page 77
Makes about 20 appetizer-size chicken pieces

6   sprigs thyme

6   leaves sage, washed and minced

1   tablespoon ground allspice

³/₄   teaspoon ground nutmeg

³/₄   teaspoon ground cinnamon

1 ¹/₂   teaspoons cayenne pepper

1 ¹/₂   teaspoons black pepper

2   tablespoons Kosher or sea salt

2 ¹/₂   tablespoons turbinado sugar

2   ounces soy sauce

6   ounces apple cider vinegar

4   ounces fresh orange juice

2   ounces fresh lime juice

2   ounces olive oil

3   cloves garlic, minced

1   cup finely chopped red onion

3   scallions, white and light green
       parts, finely chopped

1   Scotch bonnet or habanero
       pepper, seeded and finely diced,
       or ¹/₂ teaspoon Scotch bonnet
       hot sauce (found in West Indian
       markets or international sections
       of large supermarkets), optional

2   boneless chicken breasts
       (6 to 8 ounces each), skin
       removed, cut into uniform
       ¹/₄- to ¹/₂-inch chunks

Make the sauce: In a large bowl, combine the thyme, sage, allspice, nutmeg, cinnamon, peppers, salt, and sugar. In a separate bowl, whisk together the soy sauce, vinegar, orange juice, and lime juice. Add the olive oil. Pour the liquid mixture into the spices, and add the garlic, onions, scallions, and hot pepper if desired. Take out half the sauce, and put it aside to heat later as a dipping sauce.

Prepare the chicken: With a sharp knife, cut each chicken breast into ten pieces, first by cutting it in half horizontally, and then cutting each half into chunks. Place the pieces in a shallow dish, and pour half the jerk sauce over them. Cover the chicken and refrigerate for at least 30 minutes but preferably overnight. (The longer you can marinate the chicken, the more the flavor will penetrate the meat.)

To cook the chicken, in a medium-size sauté pan, sear the chunks for about 3 minutes on each side, or until cooked through. (You could also place them on an oiled baking sheet and cook in a preheated 400°F oven for 8 to 10 minutes.) In the meantime, pour the sauce you set aside into a medium-size saucepan and bring to a boil. Lower the heat, and simmer for about 15 minutes. If more liquid is needed (though you don't want it to be too runny), add some fresh orange juice. Let cool slightly and transfer to dipping bowls.

Serve the chicken immediately or at room temperature, on a platter, with a shot glass of toothpicks for serving and the extra jerk sauce for dipping.

Cucumber Raita with Coconut

Traditionally an Indian condiment, this delightful cucumber-and-yogurt-based salsa is the perfect cooling balance to spicy Caribbean dishes—though I'll eat it on its own for lunch! The kiss of coconut milk offers a lingering depth of flavor and a lovely contrast to the crunchy cucumbers. I prefer making this treat with whole-milk yogurt, but certainly you can use low fat.

See photo on page 77

Serves 8

1 ½   cups plain whole-milk (or low-fat) yogurt

    2   ounces coconut milk

        Cayenne pepper, to taste

    ½   cup coarsely chopped fresh mint

    3   cucumbers, peeled, seeded, and cut into ¼-inch cubes

    2   tablespoons shredded coconut (I like the sweetened kind,
        but unsweetened is fine too)

In a medium bowl, combine the yogurt and coconut milk. Add the pepper, then stir in the mint. Add the cucumbers. Cover and refrigerate for at least an hour. Sprinkle coconut flakes on top just before serving.

Jamaican Sorrel Punch

The leaves of the sorrel plant paint the water a deep, rich red, similar to that of a full-bodied Rioja wine. Sorrel, a type of hibiscus flower, called Jamaican flower (flor or rosa de Jamaica) in Latin American markets, has earthy, intense tones by itself, but creates an intriguingly light soda when mixed with seltzer. It's also an appetite-enhancing cocktail when mixed with rum.

Makes about 4 cups, or 8 servings

- 32 ounces water
- 1 cup dried sorrel blossoms (found in Caribbean or Latin American markets), picked over, discolored pieces discarded
- 1 tablespoon grated fresh ginger
- $1/2$ cup superfine sugar, or to taste
- 16 ounces Jamaican rum (optional)
  Half-moon lemon slices, for garnish

In a large pot, bring the water to a boil. Add the sorrel and ginger. Turn off the heat, cover, and steep for 4 hours or overnight. Strain and sweeten with sugar to taste. If serving without alcohol, add club soda to about 4 ounces of the sorrel punch. To prepare with spirits, fill a glass with ice, add 2 ounces of rum, and top with about 4 ounces of sorrel punch. Stir, garnish, and serve in a wine glass.

Mango Sangría

Sangría, the colorful wine-based drink originally from Spain, can be found in different parts of the Caribbean. Though all versions include three basic components—wine, fresh fruit, and sugar—have fun experimenting with your own favorite fruit combinations. If you want to give this one more of a punch, you can always add white rum, to taste.

Serves 4 to 6

1	bottle dry red wine
¼	cup turbinado sugar, or to taste
4	cinnamon sticks
8	ounces fresh orange juice
1	orange, peeled, seeded, and cut into thin full-moon rounds
1	lemon, peeled, seeded, and cut into thin full-moon rounds
1	mango, peeled, seeded, and cubed
1	kiwi, peeled and cut into thin rounds
1	star fruit, cut into thin slices
16	ounces seltzer

Combine the wine, sugar, and cinnamon sticks in a large pitcher. Stir until the sugar dissolves. Add the orange juice and fruit, and let rest in the refrigerator for at least 30 minutes. Before serving, add the seltzer and taste for sweetness. Serve in ice-filled wine glasses (and be sure to distribute the wine-soaked fruit).

Puerto Rican Corn Sticks (page 84) and Mango Sangría

Puerto Rican Corn Sticks

Called surullitos *in Spanish, these versatile, tasty, finger-shaped Puerto Rican snacks are addictive! People love both their texture (crunchy outside, soft inside) and flavor. They're also practical because you can make them ahead of time, then reheat them once guests have arrived. The salsita—a very simple sauce—is one version of many you might find in Puerto Rico. Of course you can adjust the heat (cayenne pepper) according to your own taste. You can also double the recipe if you're expecting a bigger crowd. The fritters combine beautifully with most cocktails, but the Ginger Lemonade (page 37) or the Dominica Lime Punch (page 76) work especially well with this appetizer.*

See photo on page 83
Makes about 18 corn sticks

Salsita

- ½ cup mayonnaise
- ½ cup ketchup
- Cayenne pepper, to taste

Fritters

- 16 ounces water
- 1 teaspoon salt
- 1 ½ cups coarse yellow cornmeal
- 1 cup grated Monterey jack, Cheddar, mozzarella, Colby, edam, *queso de papa*, or your favorite combination of cheeses (in Puerto Rico they use a cheese called *queso de bola*)
- Canola oil for frying

Make the salsita: Combine all the ingredients, cover, and refrigerate for up to 5 days.

Make the fritters: Bring the water to a boil in a medium saucepan. Add the salt. Slowly pour in the cornmeal and cook, stirring constantly, for 3 to 5 minutes, until thickened. Remove from the heat and stir in the cheese. Let the mixture rest until it's cool enough to handle. Scoop about 1 tablespoon of the dough into the palm of your hand, and shape it into an index-finger-size cylinder (about 2 inches long). Repeat with the remaining dough. At this point you can freeze the fritters or refrigerate them for up to 3 days and cook them later. (If you do freeze them, thaw fritters before cooking.)

Heat about 2 inches of oil in a skillet or deep fryer until hot but not smoking. Gently lower the fritters, one at a time, into the hot oil. Fry for 2 to 4 minutes, until golden-brown on all sides. (My first batch is usually the "throwaway" one; they taste great but the fritters don't look too good. For some reason, the second and subsequent batches come out perfectly!)

If you're not serving them immediately, set them aside and then, just prior to serving, place the fritters on baking sheets and heat in a 400°F oven until warm, about 10 minutes. Serve on a platter, with the salsita in a small dish.

Planter's Punch

Planter's Punch

Despite the many different tales about the origin of this cocktail, which stretch its birthplace from Jamaica to St. Louis, and despite the many different recipe variations found throughout the Caribbean (not to mention in Florida and other points in the States), there is one constant: It is powerful! Planter's Punch is ideally served in a tall glass with ice, topped with a bit of fresh fruit and a colorful straw. For a nonalcoholic version, add a bit more of the fresh juices and take away the rum. For a crowd, simply multiply the recipe by the number of servings and pour from an ice-filled pitcher.

Serves 1

Ice cubes

2 ounces dark rum

2 ounces fresh orange juice, plus full-moon orange slice, for garnish

2 ounces unsweetened pineapple juice

½ ounce fresh lime juice

Dash grenadine

Superfine sugar, to taste

Club soda

In a shaker filled with ice, combine the rum, the juices, and the grenadine. Shake briskly. Pour without straining into a tall glass. Top with club soda, garnish with the orange slice, and serve.

Caribbean Citrus Rum–Champagne Punch

If you've never danced the merengue, this might be what you were missing! This punch, certainly smooth and easy, can be quite powerful. Serve with bowls of Toasted Garbanzo Beans (page 30), chips, and plenty of Caribbean Guacamole (page 56).

Serves about 10

- 12 ounces fresh grapefruit juice
- 5 ounces fresh lime juice, plus 6 half-moon lime slices, for garnish
- 1/3 cup superfine sugar
- 8 ounces gold rum
- 2 ounces Cointreau or triple sec
- 1 (750-millileter) bottle Spanish cava, Prosecco, or other sparkling wine, chilled

In a large pitcher, combine the juices and the sugar. Stir briskly until the sugar is dissolved. Add the rum and orange liqueur. Chill for at least an hour or overnight. Just before serving, pour into a punch bowl and add the sparkling wine. Top with the lime slices and serve.

Caribbean-Style Tuna Salad

Called buljol, *and traditionally made with salted codfish, this variation is a light, fast, and tasty addition to any collection of cocktail snacks. Apparently the original version of this recipe also called for very hot peppers; the name* buljol *comes from French patois,* brûle gueule, *or "burn mouth." So this version is not only altered in terms of fish, it's also toned way down in terms of heat. Of course if you're up to it, you can always step up the heat. Serve on crispy lettuce leaves or on your favorite crackers, topped with fresh slices of avocado, with Ginger-Champagne Cocktails (page 40), Passion Fruit Cocktails Caribbean Style (page 65), or Dominica Lime Punch (page 76).*

Serves about 10

2   six-ounce cans tuna in
        water, drained
1   medium onion, finely chopped
3   medium tomatoes, chopped
1   Scotch bonnet, habanero, or
        jalapeño pepper
        (or to taste), finely diced
3   tablespoons olive oil
2   hard-boiled eggs, peeped
        and chopped (optional)

2   ounces fresh lime juice
1   red bell pepper, finely chopped
    Kosher salt (use less salt if serving
        on salty crackers)
    Freshly ground black pepper,
        to taste
2   ripe avocados, seeded and sliced
        (just before serving)
    Lettuce leaves or crackers
        for serving

In a large bowl, combine all of the ingredients except the avocado, lettuce, or crackers. Cover and chill for at least an hour or even overnight. Set the lettuce or crackers on a serving tray, and spoon a small amount of tuna salad on each piece. Top with an appropriate-size slice of avocado (it shouldn't be bigger than the lettuce or cracker!) and serve.

Bajan Punch and Black-Eyed Pea Fritters (page 92)

Bajan Punch

The word punch *comes from the Hindustani (Hindi and Urdu) word* panch, *which means "five," and refers to five key ingredients originally used in the drink: tea, arrack (strong spirits distilled chiefly in Asia from fermented fruits, grains, or sugarcane), sugar, lemons, and water. Thanks to English colonists, the drink traveled from India westward, where it has taken on many new lives! According to my Grenada-born and -raised neighbor Paula—who has graciously shared her recipes and palate with me—this Bajan rum punch follows the Caribbean "rule of five" for rum punches: 1. sour (lime juice); 2. sweet (sugar); 3. strong (rum); 4. weak (water); and 5. nutmeg. Of course, versions of rum punch abound throughout the region and vary according to island and bartender. Sample liberally to find what you like best! Serve this punch with Pumpkin Fritters (page 106) and Jamaican Jerk Chicken (page 78).*

Serves 10 to 12

2 cups granulated sugar	24 ounces dark rum
16 ounces cold water	2 dashes Angostura bitters
8 ounces fresh lime juice, plus 24 half-moon lime slices, for garnish	4 cups crushed ice
	Ground nutmeg

Put the sugar in a small saucepan, add the 2 cups of water and bring to a boil, stirring constantly. Lower the heat and simmer for 3 to 5 minutes, until the sugar is completely dissolved. Remove from the heat and cool.

Pour the resulting syrup into a large container. Add the lime juice and rum. Add the bitters and mix once more before chilling for at least an hour. Combine in a pitcher or bowl with the crushed ice, add lime slices, top with a sprinkle of nutmeg, and serve.

Black-Eyed Pea Fritters

I first had black-eyed pea fritters in Brazil (where they're popular in Bahia and called acaraje*), which is just many of the places this West African–born dish landed in the New World. Found in different versions throughout the Caribbean, this one has been adapted with canned black-eyed peas, though, of course, you can use them dry and soak them overnight before cooking. These are best served hot, golden, and crispy on the outside and soft in the center (though you can reheat them in a 400°F for about 10 minutes).*

See photo on page 90

Makes about 30 fritters

1   cup cooked (or 1 15-ounce can, strained and rinsed) black-eyed peas
1   Scotch bonnet chile, seeded and minced, or 1 teaspoon Scotch bonnet hot
       sauce (found in West Indian markets or international sections of large
       supermarkets), or 2 jalapeño peppers, seeded and chopped (optional)
2   scallions, white and light green parts, chopped
1   clove garlic, finely chopped
1   red bell pepper, finely chopped
1   egg
1 3/4 cups all-purpose flour
       Kosher salt and freshly ground black pepper, to taste
2   tablespoons coarsely chopped flat-leaf parsley, plus additional for garnish
       Vegetable oil for frying

In a food processor, combine the peas, chile or hot sauce, scallions, garlic, and half the minced red bell pepper, and process just until smooth. Add the egg. Gradually add the flour, salt, and pepper, and mix just until well blended. Stir in the remaining red pepper and 1 tablespoon of the chopped parsley.

Heat about 1 inch of oil in a heavy frying pan. Pick up the dough by tablespoons or put a bit of oil on your hands, rub them together, and form the dough into pancakes about 1 inch wide and $1/4$ inch thick. Repeat with the remaining dough.

At this point you can cover the fritters and store them in the refrigerator (for up to 2 days) or start frying. Add the patties, a few at a time without crowding, and cook for about 3 minutes on each side, or until golden-brown. Drain on paper towels, sprinkle with the remaining parsley, and serve immediately.

Caribe Cocktail Punch

Puerto Viejo—the beach town located on the Caribbean side of Costa Rica—not only offers gorgeous beaches and wonderful people, it also serves a great selection of cocktails! This is a re-creation of the Caribe Cocktail I sampled there. It's a bit different from the others I'd tried, mostly because of the addition of passion fruit juice—which complements the pineapple juice and rum beautifully. This recipe is great for a crowd; you can prepare the juice combination ahead of time, then add the rum and ice when your guests have arrived. This recipe can easily be doubled for an even bigger crowd.

Serves approximately 10

15 ounces white rum
15 ounces passion fruit nectar
10 ounces unsweetened pineapple juice
 1 fresh pineapple, cubed, plus 2 wedges, for garnish
 2 ounces fresh lime juice
 5 ounces mango nectar
    Superfine sugar, to taste
 5 cups ice cubes

In a large bowl, combine the rum, passion fruit nectar, pineapple juice, pineapple, lime juice, and mango nectar. Taste and add sugar if desired. Cover and refrigerate until ready to serve. Prior to serving, combine half the juice mixture with $2\frac{1}{2}$ cups of the ice in a blender and process until smooth. Repeat with the remaining ingredients. Pour into a glass pitcher or right into chilled wine glasses. Garnish and serve immediately.

Caribe Cocktail Punch and Sweet Plantains Wrapped in Bacon (page 96)

Sweet Plantains Wrapped in Bacon

The contrast between the sweetness of the plantains and the saltiness of the bacon—as well as the contrasting textures—make this very easy appetizer quite addictive. Use ripe plantains—ones whose skins have begun to blacken and that feel soft to the touch. Serve with Caribe Cocktail Punch (page 94), Dominican Hurricane (page 20), Orange Daiquiri (page 32), or any cocktail you choose!

See photo on page 95

Makes 20 individual servings

  2 very ripe (almost black) plantains
10 slices bacon (preferably thick)

Preheat the oven to 400°F.

Line a baking sheet with aluminum foil. Peel the plantains and slice them in medallions on a slight diagonal. Cut the bacon slices in half. Wrap each medallion, horizontally, with a bacon slice (or you can slice them into rounds; as in the picture on page 95) and wrap the bacon around the rims. Place the wrapped plantain slices on the ungreased foil. (At this point you can refrigerate the tray until ready to bake.)

Bake in the preheated oven for about 12 minutes (about 6 minutes on each side), or until the bacon is crispy and the plantains are soft. Serve on a platter and give your guests the option of using their fingers or toothpicks to retrieve their treats.

Panamanian Papaya Punch

Panama is a small country with a "big" location. It's an isthmus that not only connects South America (Colombia) to Central America (Costa Rica), but also the North Pacific Ocean to the Caribbean Sea. Like other Caribbean-rimmed areas, Panama boasts a treasure chest of cultural influences visible in everything from its art—as in molas (gorgeously colorful quiltlike tapestries made by the Cuna Indians of the San Blas Islands) to its cuisine and cocktails—as in this Chicha de Papaya, or Papaya Punch. Enjoy with Panamanian Ceviche (page 99), or any appetizer you choose.

See photo on page 98
Serves 8 to 10

2	cups papaya, peeled, seeded, and diced
8	ounces unsweetened pineapple juice
2	ounces fresh lime or lemon juice
10	ounces papaya nectar
16	ounces white rum
1	cup ice cubes
16	ounces sparkling water or lemon-lime soda

In a blender, combine the fresh papaya, pineapple juice, lime or lemon juice, and papaya nectar. Add the rum; you may want to blend in batches. Taste and adjust the flavors (you may want to add more of one of the juices—or maybe more rum!). Pour into a pitcher and add the sparkling water or lemon-lime soda. Serve in glasses over ice.

Panamanian Papaya Punch (page 97) and Ceviche

Panamanian Ceviche

Most Latin American countries have their versions of this Peruvian- or Ecuadorian-born treat. Though the ingredients can vary, it's crucial that they be as fresh as possible. This is a great summer-barbecue appetizer that goes well with Panamanian Papaya Punch (page 97), Pineapple Martini (page 55), Passion Fruit Cocktail Caribbean Style (page 65), or just about any fruity drink you're in the mood for!

Makes 4 to 6 appetizer servings

- 1 pound boneless sea bass *(corvina)*, red snapper, or any good-quality white fish
- 1 1/2 cups finely chopped red onion
- 10 1/2 ounces fresh lime juice
- 1/2 cup finely chopped celery
- 1/4 cup finely chopped fresh cilantro
- 1/2 Scotch bonnet or jalapeño pepper, finely minced (optional)
- Salt, to taste
- Endive leaves or red-leaf lettuce
- Saltines

Cut the fish into bite-size pieces and place them in a glass bowl or dish that's at least 2 inches high. In a separate bowl, combine the onion, lime juice, celery, cilantro, and hot pepper as desired. Pour the mixture on top of the fish; it should cover the fish. Add salt to taste. Cover with plastic wrap and place in the refrigerator for at least 4 hours (or until the fish starts to turn opaque) or up to 12. Serve in endive leaves or small lettuce-layered dishes, with crackers or Saltines.

Anguilla Fruit Punch

During the past couple of decades, the thin 16-mile long island of Anguilla (whose name means "eel" in Italian!) has become a popular vacation destination for scores of visitors. It is home to many gorgeous white-sand beaches, including Shoal Bay East, one of the finest in the eastern Caribbean, known for its relaxed tropical lifestyle. The island now boasts more than 80 restaurants, which feature—as is the case in many Caribbean locations—a bold combination of flavors. This powerful punch goes really well with Jamaican Jerk Chicken (page 78), Puerto Rican Corn Sticks (page 84), and Juanita's Yuca Fritters (page 22), among others.

Serves 10 to 12

- 24 ounces golden rum
- 3 ounces Amaretto
- 16 ounces unsweetened pineapple juice
- 16 ounces fresh orange juice, plus about 12 half-moon orange slices, for garnish
- 8 ounces guava nectar
- 6 dashes Angostura bitters
- 4 ounces grenadine
- 4 ounces fresh lime juice

Combine all of the ingredients, except the orange slices, in a large punch bowl or pitcher. Chill for at least an hour. Serve over ice, garnished with the orange slices.

Milk—and cream—pour easily into cocktails. Deftly counterbalanced with the punch of alcohol, these sleek treats can be light enough to marry with your preferred treats, yet hefty enough to be a meal all on their own. Find your favorites, and spread the wealth. . . .

SILKY & SPIRITED

102 Rum & Coconut Milk Punch

103 Jamaican Carrot Cocktail

104 Jamaican Banana Cooler

106 Pumpkin Fritters

109 Soursop *(Guanábana)* Cocktail

110 Dominican Summertime Drink

111 Guava-Coconut Smoothie

112 Crème de Cacao & Vodka Shake

114 Puerto Rican Egg Nog *(Coquito)*

115 Bushwacker

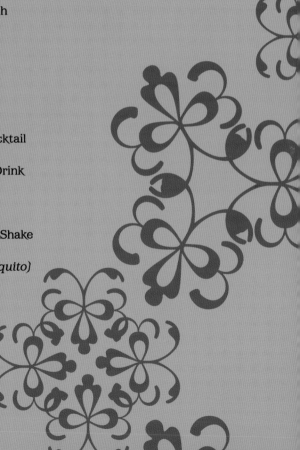

Rum & Coconut Milk Punch

Incarnations of this nutmeg-flecked, fresh snowy-white drink can be found throughout the islands. You may want to make this more of a milkshake; to do so, simply combine all the ingredients in a blender. For a large crowd, just multiply by the number of people, but do make adjustments for sweetness; you may want to go easier on the coconut cream (in fact, I like it without the added cream of coconut) and then use the sweetened or toasted coconut flakes. Serve with Costa Rican–Style Corn Cakes (page 62) topped with Mango Chutney (page 64).

Serves 1

- 2 ounces white rum
- 4 ounces coconut milk
- $\frac{1}{2}$ teaspoon coconut cream, or to taste
- 1 splash vanilla extract
-    Ice cubes
-    Sweetened or unsweetened coconut flakes, toasted, for garnish
-    Nutmeg, for garnish

Combine all of the ingredients, except the coconut flakes and nutmeg, in a shaker filled with ice. Shake briskly, pour into a glass, garnish, and serve. You can also strain into a chilled martini glass, garnish, and serve.

Jamaican Carrot Cocktail

Carrot juice is not for everyone. When I gave this to my teenage daughter to try, she told me, "It's very good, but I'm not a carrot-juice person!" However, if you are a fan of this healthful orange veggie, you'll enjoy this almost dessertlike—and very refreshing—drink, which can be made with or without the added kick of rum.

Serves 2

- 16 ounces excellent-quality chilled carrot juice (available in large markets and in health food stores)
- 2 ounces sweetened condensed milk
- 1/4 teaspoon ground nutmeg
- 1/4 teaspoon vanilla extract
  - White rum, to taste (optional)
- 1 cup crushed ice
  - Ground cinnamon, to sprinkle on top

In a blender, combine the carrot juice, condensed milk, nutmeg, vanilla, and rum, if desired. Process until well blended. Serve immediately or refrigerate until ready. Pour into two glasses with 1/2 cup each of crushed ice. Garnish with cinnamon and serve.

Jamaican Banana Cooler

The first time I ever saw bananas growing was in Jamaica, when I was a little girl. The plants—which appeared to have Dr. Seuss–like leaves that sheltered what looked like hundreds of banana bunches—were unforgettable. This cocktail, which is more like a dessert than an appetite enhancer, is just one example of many of the beautiful island's incorporation of the delicious fruit into drinks and food. Though this drink is rich enough be served on its own, hot Pumpkin Fritters (page 106) offer a nice side treat.

Serves 2

- 2 ounces light rum
- 1 ounce clear crème de cacao
- 1 ounce half-and-half
- 2 scoops vanilla ice cream
- 1 very ripe banana (the riper, the better!)
- 1 cup ice cubes
- 1 tablespoon shaved dark chocolate, for garnish
- 2 cinnamon sticks, for garnish

Combine all of the ingredients, except the chocolate and cinnamon sticks, in a blender and process until smooth. Pour into two chilled wine glasses. Sprinkle the chocolate on top, add the cinnamon sticks (optional), and serve.

Pumpkin Fritters (page 106) and Jamaican Banana Cooler

Pumpkin Fritters

These addictive puffs of pumpkin, which are a slight variation on a classic Bajan recipe, are slightly crispy on the outside—and melt-in-your-mouth soft on the inside. (My daughter, Sofia, says they're "amazing!") Though they're a bit uneven looking—since it's hard to form this batter into a perfect ball—they'll win you and your guests over at first bite. They are sweet, so you can balance them with another appetizer that's not, such as Jamaican Jerk Chicken (page 78). Serve them with Ginger Lemonade (page 37), Jamaican Sorrel Punch (page 81), or just about any light and fruity cocktail.

See photo on page 105

Makes about 12 fritters

1	(15-ounce) can pumpkin (*not* pumpkin pie filler)
½	cup all-purpose flour
1	egg
¼	cup turbinado sugar
½	teaspoon salt
1	teaspoon baking powder
1	teaspoon ground cinnamon
½	teaspoon ground allspice
¼	teaspoon ground nutmeg
	Canola oil, for frying
	Confectioners' sugar, for garnish

In a large bowl, combine all of the ingredients, except the oil and sugar. Mix just until blended. Pour the oil to a depth of 1 inch into a deep, heavy skillet. Test the oil for hotness by dropping a small bit of batter into it; it should rise pretty quickly.

Drop the batter by teaspoonfuls into the hot oil, being careful not to crowd the skillet. After the bottoms start to brown, turn the fritters over so they brown evenly. (They cook very quickly—in 1 to 3 minutes.) Drain well on paper towels.

Serve immediately (or reheat in a 400°F oven for about 10 minutes). Sprinkle sugar on top just prior to serving.

Soursop *(Guanábana)* Cocktail

Soursop (Guanábana) Cocktail

The first time I had this prehistoric-on-the-outside but silky-sexy-on-the-inside fruit was in Peru (where it's called chirimoya*). It's hard not to be seduced by the soft, fragrant flavors of this tropical fruit, which grows throughout the Caribbean. Though I enjoyed this cocktail in Limón, Costa Rica, where they claim it came from Jamaica, it's also served in Puerto Rico and Cuba, where it's called Champola. This milky cocktail could also be called a Caribbean White Russian! Serve any time, well chilled and over crushed ice.*

Serves 2

- 32 ounces soursop nectar (available at Latin markets and Caribbean
      grocery stores)
- 4 ounces rum
- 1/2 teaspoon grated lime zest, or more to taste
- 1/2 teaspoon ground nutmeg, plus additional, for garnish
- 6 ounces sweetened condensed milk, or to taste
- 1 cup crushed ice

Combine the nectar, rum, lime zest, nutmeg, and about 1/2 cup of the sweetened condensed milk. Taste and add more milk if desired. Chill for at least an hour and up to a day before serving. After pouring the mixture on top of crushed ice, add a sprinkle of nutmeg and more lime zest, as desired.

Dominican Summertime Drink

Called morir soñando—*or "to die dreaming"—in Spanish, this nonalcoholic treat may have been inspired by the poem* Morir Soñando, *the last poem written by the famous nineteenth-century Spanish poet and philosopher Miguel de Unamuno, or perhaps by the idyllic scenery that the Dominican Republic has to offer. Cool and tasty, this creamy mixture is reminiscent of a creamsicle, which offers that same contrast of sweet and creamy. To prevent curdling, make sure both the orange juice and the milk are quite cold.*

Serves 4

- 32 ounces chilled evaporated milk
- ½ cup superfine sugar
- 2 cups ice cubes
- 16 ounces fresh orange juice, well chilled, plus 1 teaspoon grated orange rind, for garnish (optional)

Combine the milk and sugar and mix well. Chill for at least 2 hours (the milk needs to be very cold), or up to a day. In a blender, combine the ice and milk. Slowly add the orange juice. Garnish and serve immediately.

Guava-Coconut Smoothie

These two flavors are synonymous with tropical. This is a great summertime cocktail (though it can bring you summer in chilly northern areas) that marries well with Jamaican Jerk Chicken (page 78), Salmon Patties (page 42), and Puerto Rican Corn Sticks (page 84). Of course you can also make it for the nonalcohol drinking crowd by simply omitting the rum and adding more nectar or milk, according to taste.

Serves 2 to 4

- 8 ounces white or gold rum
- 8 ounces guava nectar
- 1 ounce cream of coconut
- 1 teaspoon vanilla extract
- 3 ounces unsweetened pineapple juice
- 1 cup vanilla ice cream
- 2 cups ice cubes
  Sweetened coconut flakes, for garnish
  Grated nutmeg, for garnish

In a blender, combine the rum, guava nectar, and cream of coconut. Add the vanilla, pineapple juice, ice cream, and ice, and blend until smooth. Garnish and serve in chilled glasses.

Crème de Cacao & Vodka Shake

Cacao, or chocolate bean, grows throughout the Caribbean. It's an interesting-looking tree, and the cacao pods—which are oval and about the size of large papayas—look as if they're barely hanging on by the thin little stems that attach them to the bark of the trees. Crème de cacao is a cacao-flavored liqueur that is usually less sweet and syrupy than its cousin, chocolate liqueur. Though it comes in clear and dark-brown versions, I find the lighter one works better in this drink. Served in a wine glass with a sprinkle of cinnamon, this snow-white cocktail may be more of a post- than pre-dinner treat. Try serving these adult milk shakes to cool down the spark of spicy Jamaican Jerk Chicken (page 78).

Serves 4

- 4 tablespoons sweetened condensed milk
- 4 ounces vodka
- 2 ounces clear crème de cacao
- 4 cups ice cubes
  Ground cinnamon, for garnish

Combine all of the ingredients, except the cinnamon, in a blender and process until smooth. Pour into wine glasses, sprinkle with ground cinnamon, and serve.

Crème de Cacao & Vodka Shake

Puerto Rican Egg Nog (Coquito)

Every Puerto Rican family has its own version of this Christmastime cocktail, whose Spanish name means "little coconut" in English. And though families may argue about the ingredients, they all agree on one thing: Coquito *must be served cold. This is typically served in small glasses.*

Makes 4 to 6 servings

8 ounces water
3 cinnamon sticks
3 cloves
4 egg yolks
1 (12-ounce) can evaporated milk
1 (14-ounce) can sweetened
    condensed milk

1 (14-ounce) can coconut milk
8 ounces white rum
1 teaspoon vanilla extract
    Ground cinnamon and/or
      nutmeg, for garnish

In a small saucepan, bring the water to a boil. Add the cinnamon sticks and cloves and simmer for about 10 minutes, or until the water is reduced by about half. Set aside to cool. When the cinnamon water has cooled, remove the cinnamon sticks and cloves.

Meanwhile, in a medium saucepan or the top of a double boiler, whisk together the egg yolks and evaporated milk and cook for about 10 minutes, stirring constantly (without boiling) until the mixture coats a spoon. Set aside to cool.

In a blender (you may have to do this in batches), combine the cooled cinnamon water, egg yolk mixture, remaining milks, rum, and vanilla. Chill well (for at least an hour). Serve, sprinkled with cinnamon and nutmeg on top.

Bushwacker

This cocktail, called the official drink of St. Thomas, is like a power-packed milk shake (and should probably be called ambusher *because of how it sneaks up on you)! Though there are many versions of this adult treat found in St. Thomas (and also in Florida), most include rum, Tía María or Kahlúa, and cream.*

Serves 2

- 3   ounces Tía María (or Kahlúa)
- 1   ounce light rum
- 1   ounce clear crème de cacao
- 4   ounces cream of coconut
- 4   ounces milk or half-and-half
- 2   cups ice cubes
  Ground nutmeg, for garnish

Combine all of the ingredients, except for the nutmeg, in a blender and process until smooth. Pour into chilled wine or cocktail glasses, sprinkle with nutmeg, and serve.

ACKNOWLEDGMENTS

Thanks to my super agent, Jane Dystel; my fabulous Jennifers: editors Jennifer Levesque and Jennifer Eiss—as well as the rest of the team at STC; the amazingly talented designer, Lana Lê; and the fabulous photographer, Ellie Miller, and her great group—including fantastic food stylist Sara Neumeier. Thanks also to my wonderful family—especially my parents Tony and Sonia Gargagliano, my father-in-law Lionel Markusfeld, and my sister-in-law Chef Amy Magee, as well as my Glenwood Lake neighbors and much-beloved friends who never ceased to offer their support and tasting services, as well as their honest comments and suggestions. *Muchísimas gracias a Wady, Vivian—y toda la familia Gutiérrez-Vargas en Costa Rica por presentarme a Danny Hayling y su Tía Ester.* Special thanks to *mi querido amigo* and traveling partner, Christian Foucher, who brought me to meet his beautiful and loving *familia dominicana,* headed by one of the most extraordinary home cooks I've ever met, Juanita. And finally, thank you so very much to all my ESL students, past and present, who continue to amaze me with their courage, enthusiasm, and love of life.

CONVERSION CHARTS

The weights and measurements given below are not exact equivalents but have been rounded up or down slightly to make measuring easier.

weight equivalents

AVOIRDUPOIS	METRIC
$1/4$ oz	7 g
$1/2$ oz	15 g
1 oz	30 g
2 oz	60 g
3 oz	90 g
4 oz	115 g
5 oz	150 g
6 oz	175 g
7 oz	200 g
8 oz ($1/2$ lb)	25 g
9 oz	250 g
10 oz	300 g
11 oz	325 g
12 oz	350 g
13 oz	375 g
14 oz	400 g
15 oz	425 g
16 oz (1 lb)	450 g
$1 1/2$ lb	750 g
2 lb	900 g
$2 1/4$ lb	1.0 kg
3 lb	1.4 kg
4 lb	1.8 kg

volume equivalents

AMERICAN	METRIC	IMPERIAL
$1/4$ t	1.2 ml	
$1/2$ t	2.5 ml	
1 t	5.0 ml	
$1/2$ T (1.5 t)	7.5 ml	
1 T (3 t)	15 ml	
$1/4$ cup (4 T)	60 ml	2 fl oz
$1/3$ cup (5 T)	75 ml	$2 1/2$ fl oz
$1/2$ cup (8 T)	125 ml	4 fl oz
$2/3$ cup (10 T)	150 ml	5 fl oz
$3/4$ cup (12 T)	175 ml	6 fl oz
1 cup (16 T)	250 ml	8 fl oz
$1 1/4$ cups	300 ml	10 fl oz ($1/2$ pt)
$1 1/2$ cups	350 ml	12 fl oz
2 cups (1 pint)	500 ml	16 fl oz
$2 1/2$ cups	625 ml	20 fl oz (1 pint)
1 quart	1 liter	32 fl oz

oven temperature equivalents

OVEN MARK	F	C	GAS
Very cool	250–275	130–140	$1/2$–1
Cool	300	150	2
Warm	325	170	3
Moderate	350	180	4
Moderately hot	375	190	5
	400	200	6
Hot	425	220	7
	450	230	8
Very hot	475	250	9

INDEX

Anguillan Fruit Punch, 100
Appetizers
    black-eyed pea fritters,
        92–93
    Caribbean guacamole, 56
    Caribbean-style tuna
        salad, 89
    carrot & raisin salad, 67
    codfish cakes, 74–75
    Costa Rican green plantain
        appetizer, 38–39
    Costa Rican-style corn
        cakes (arepas), 62–63
    cucumber raita with
        coconut, 80
    Jamaican banana fritters,
        36
    Jamaican jerk chicken,
        78–79
    Juanita's yuca fritters,
        22–23
    mango chutney, 64
    okra polenta, 46–47
    Panamanian ceviche, 99
    Puerto Rican corn sticks,
        84–85
    pumpkin fritters, 106–7
    salmon patties, 42–43
    sweet plantains wrapped
        in bacon, 96
    toasted garbanzo beans,
        30
    tostones, 14
Arepas (Costa Rican-Style
    Corn Cakes), 62–63
Avocados
    Caribbean guacamole, 56

Bahama Mama, 18
Baja
    pumpkin fritters, 106–7
    punch, 91
Banana
    colada, 59
    cooler, Jamaican, 104
    daiquiri, 28
    fritters, Jamaican, 36
Beans, Garbanzo, Toasted,
    30
Beer, Ginger, 48
Beer Cooler, Jamaican, 49
Belize Cocktail, 13
Bermuda
    dark & stormy, 17
Black-Eyed Pea Fritters,
    92–93
Blue Mountain Cocktail, 16
Brown Cow, 25
Bushwacker, 115

Caribbean cocktails, classic,
    11–26
Caribbean-fruit cocktails,
    58–70. See also Martini
Caribe Cocktail Punch, 94
Carrot Cocktail, Jamaican,
    103
Carrot & Raisin Salad, 67
Ceviche, Panamanian, 99
Champagne
    cocktail, sorrel, 73
    -ginger cocktail, 40
    -rum citrus punch,
        Caribbean, 88
Chicken, Jamaican Jerk,
    78–79
Chutney, Mango, 64

Coconut
    banana colada, 59
    Bushwacker, 115
    cucumber raita with, 80
    -guava smoothie, 111
    martini, 53
    milk & rum punch, 102
    water & gin, 58
Coconut rum
    Bahama Mama, 18
    Belize cocktail, 13
    Caribbean cosmopolitan,
        60
    papapa flower, 68
Codfish Cakes, 74–75
Coffee liqueur
    brown cow, 25
    Bushwacker, 115
Cointreau
    Caribbean cosmopolitan,
        60
    El Presidente, 15
    frozen daiquiri, 33
    Spanish Town cocktail, 26
Coquito (Puerto Rican Egg
    Nog), 114
Corn Cakes, Costa Rican-
    Style (Arepas), 62–63
Corn Sticks, Puerto Rican,
    84–85
Cosmopolitan, Caribbean,
    60
Costa Rica
    Caribe cocktail punch, 94
    green plantain appetizer,
        38–39
    -style corn cakes
        (arepas), 62–63

Crème de cacao
Bushwacker, 115
& vodka shake, 112
Cuba
El Presidente, 15
frozen daiquiri, 33
Cucumber Raita with
Coconut, 80
Curaçao Cocktail, 70

Daiquiri
banana, 28
frozen, 33
guava, 35
papaya, 31
Dark & Stormy, 17
Dominican Republic
hurricane, 20
lime punch, 76
rum sour, 24
summertime drink, 110
tostones, 14

Egg Nog, Puerto Rican
(Coquito), 114
El Presidente, 15

Fish
Caribbean-style tuna
salad, 89
codfish cakes, 74-75
Panamanian ceviche, 99
salmon patties, 42-43
Fritters
banana, Jamaican, 36
black-eyed pea, 92-93
Puerto Rican corn sticks,
84-85
pumpkin, 106-7
yuca, Juanita's, 22-23
Frozen Daiquiri. 33

Garbanzo Beans, Toasted, 30
Gin & Coconut Water, 58
Ginger
beer, 48
-Champagne cocktail, 40
dark & stormy, 17
lemonade, 37
Guacamole, Caribbean, 56
Guanábana (Soursop)
Cocktail, 109
Guava
Anguillan fruit punch, 100
-coconut smoothie, 111
daiquiri, 35

Jamaica
banana cooler, 104
banana fritters, 36
beer cooler, 49
Blue Mountain cocktail, 16
brown cow, 25
carrot cocktail, 103
jerk chicken, 78-79
sorrel punch, 81
Spanish Town cocktail, 26
Jerk Chicken, Jamaican,
78-79

Lemon
ginger-Champagne
cocktail, 40
ginger lemonade, 37
Virgin Island cooler, 50
Lemonade, Ginger, 37
Lime
Bajan punch, 91
banana daiquiri, 28
Caribbean citrus rum-
Champagne punch, 88
Caribbean cosmopolitan,
60
frozen daiquiri, 33
guava daiquiri, 35
orange daiquiri, 32

Panamanian ceviche, 99
papaya daiquiri, 31
punch, Dominica, 76

Mandarin Orange Cocktail,
45
Mango
chutney, 64
Curaçao cocktail, 70
martini, 57
sangría, 82
Martini
coconut, 53
mango, 57
pineapple, 55
sorrel, 54

Okra Polenta, 46-47
Orange(s)
Anguillan fruit punch, 100
Blue Mountain cocktail, 16
daiquiri, 32
Dominican summertime
drink, 110
mandarin, cocktail, 45
mango sangría, 82
planter's punch, 87
rum shrub, 19
Virgin Island cooler, 50

Panamanian Papaya Punch,
97
Papaya
Caribbean guacamole, 56
daiquiri, 31
flower, 68
punch, Panamanian, 97
Passion Fruit
Caribe cocktail punch, 94
cocktail Caribbean style,
65

Pineapple
  Anguillan fruit punch, 100
  Bahama Mama, 18
  banana colada, 59
  Belize cocktail, 13
  Caribe cocktail punch, 94
  Jamaican beer cooler, 49
  martini, 55
  Panamanian papaya
    punch, 97
  planter's punch, 87
Plantain(s)
  green, appetizer, Costa
    Rican, 38–39
  sweet, wrapped in bacon,
    96
  tostones, 14
Planter's Punch, 87
Polenta, Okra, 46–47
Puerto Rican Corn Sticks,
  84–85
Puerto Rican Egg Nog
  (Coquito), 114
Pumpkin Fritters, 106–7
Punch, 71–100

Raita, Cucumber, with
  Coconut, 80
Rum
  Anguillan fruit punch, 100
  Bahama Mama, 18
  Bajan punch, 91
  banana colada, 59
  banana daiquiri, 28
  Belize cocktail, 13
  Blue Mountain cocktail, 16
  Bushwacker, 115
  Caribbean cosmopolitan,
    60
  Caribe cocktail punch, 94

  -Champagne punch,
    Caribbean citrus, 88
  & coconut milk punch,
    102
  Curaçao cocktail, 70
  dark & stormy, 17
  Dominica lime punch, 76
  Dominican hurricane, 20
  El Presidente, 15
  frozen daiquiri, 33
  guava-coconut smoothie,
    111
  guava daiquiri, 35
  Jamaican banana cooler,
    104
  Jamaican beer cooler, 49
  Jamaican sorrel punch, 81
  mandarin orange cocktail,
    45
  orange daiquiri, 32
  Panamanian papaya
    punch, 97
  papapa flower, 68
  papaya daiquiri, 31
  passion fruit cocktail
    Caribbean style, 65
  planter's punch, 87
  Puerto Rican egg nog
    (coquito), 114
  shrub, 19
  sour, 24
  soursop (guanábana)
    cocktail, 109
  Spanish Town cocktail, 26
  Virgin Island cooler, 50

Salmon Patties, 42–43
Sangría, Mango, 82
Silky & spirited cocktails,
  101–15
Smoothie, Guava-Coconut,
  111

Sorrel
  Champagne cocktail, 73
  martini, 54
  punch, Jamaican, 81
Soursop (Guanábana)
  Cocktail, 109
Spanish Town Cocktail, 26

Tostones, 14
Trinidad
  ginger lemonade, 37
  toasted garbanzo beans,
    30
Tropical-infused cocktails,
  37–50. See also Daiquiri
Tuna Salad, Caribbean-Style,
  89

Virgin Island Cooler, 50
Vodka
  coconut martini, 53
  & crème de cacao shake,
    112
  ginger lemonade, 37
  mango martini, 57
  pineapple martini, 55
  sorrel martini, 54

Wine
  Caribbean citrus rum-
    Champagne punch, 88
  ginger-Champagne
    cocktail, 40
  mango sangría, 82
  sorrel Champagne
    cocktail, 73

Yuca Fritters, Juanita's,
  22–23